WEATHERPROOFING

Other Publications:

UNDERSTANDING COMPUTERS
YOUR HOME
THE ENCHANTED WORLD
THE KODAK LIBRARY OF CREATIVE PHOTOGRAPHY
GREAT MEALS IN MINUTES
THE CIVIL WAR
PLANET EARTH
COLLECTOR'S LIBRARY OF THE CIVIL WAR
THE EPIC OF FLIGHT
THE GOOD COOK
THE SEAFARERS
WORLD WAR II
THE OLD WEST

For information on and a full description of any of the
Time-Life Books series listed above, please write:

Reader Information
Time-Life Books
541 North Fairbanks Court
Chicago, Illinois 60611

This volume is part of a series offering homeowners
detailed instructions on repairs, construction
and improvements they can undertake themselves.

HOME REPAIR
AND IMPROVEMENT

WEATHERPROOFING

BY THE EDITORS OF
TIME-LIFE BOOKS

TIME-LIFE BOOKS
ALEXANDRIA, VIRGINIA

Time-Life Books Inc.
is a wholly owned subsidiary of
TIME INCORPORATED

Founder   Henry R. Luce 1898-1967

Editor-in-Chief   Henry Anatole Grunwald
President   J. Richard Munro
Chairman of the Board   Ralph P. Davidson
Corporate Editor   Jason McManus
Group Vice President, Books   Reginald K. Brack Jr.
Vice President, Books   George Artandi

TIME-LIFE BOOKS INC.

Editor   George Constable
Executive Editor   George Daniels
Editorial General Manager   Neal Goff
Director of Design   Louis Klein
Editorial Board   Dale M. Brown, Roberta Conlan, Ellen Phillips,
                Gerry Schremp, Donia Ann Steele, Rosalind Stubenberg,
                Kit van Tulleken, Henry Woodhead
Director of Research   Phyllis K. Wise
Director of Photography   John Conrad Weiser

President   William J. Henry
Senior Vice President   Christopher T. Linen
Vice Presidents   Stephen L. Bair, Edward Brash, Robert A. Ellis,
                John M. Fahey Jr., Juanita T. James,
                James L. Mercer, Wilhelm R. Saake, Paul R. Stewart,
                Leopoldo Toralballa

HOME REPAIR AND IMPROVEMENT

Editorial Staff for Weatherproofing

Editor   William Frankel
Assistant Editor   Lee Hassig
Designer   Herbert H. Quarmby
Picture Editor   Kay Neil Noble
Associate Designer   Robert McKee
Staff Writers   Jane Alexander, Helen Barer, Marilyn Bethany,
                Sally French, Simone D. Gossner, Lee Greene,
                Michael Luftman, Brian McGinn, Joan Mebane,
                James Murphy, Don Nelson
Copy Coordinators   Ricki Tarlow, Eleanor Van Bellingham
Art Associates   Richard Salcer, Victoria Vebell, Mary B. Wilshire
Editorial Assistant   Eleanor G. Kask

Editorial Operations
Design   Ellen Robling (assistant director)
Copy Chief   Diane Ullius
Editorial Operations   Caroline A. Boubin (manager)
Production   Celia Beattie
Quality Control   James J. Cox (director)
Library   Louise D. Forstall

Correspondents: Elisabeth Kraemer-Singh (Bonn);
Margot Hapgood, Dorothy Bacon (London); Miriam
Hsia, Lucy T. Voulgaris (New York); Maria Vincenza
Aloisi, Josephine du Brusle (Paris); Ann Natanson (Rome).
Valuable assistance was also provided by: Judy Aspinall,
Karin B. Pearce (London); Carolyn T. Chubet, Christina
Lieberman (New York); Mimi Murphy (Rome).

THE CONSULTANTS: Lelland L. Gallup is Assistant
Professor of Housing and Design at New York State
College of Human Ecology, Cornell University, Itha-
ca, New York. He is responsible for a series of innova-
tive home-maintenance courses given to New York
state homeowners and home associations, and has
written numerous articles on home repair.

Harris Mitchell, special consultant for Canada, has
been working in the field of home repair and improvement for more than two decades. He is Homes
editor of Today magazine and author of a syndicated
newspaper column, "You Wanted to Know," as well
as several books on home improvement.

Clifford A. Wojan, formerly Professor of Mechanical
Engineering at the Polytechnic Institute of New York,
is a consulting engineer in thermal engineering. In
that capacity, he regularly advises industry and government on heating and cooling installations, insulation and energy conservation.

Time-Life Books Inc. offers a wide range of fine recordings,
including a Rock 'n' Roll Era series. For subscription information, call 1-800-621-7026 or write Time-Life Music, P.O. Box
C-32068, Richmond, Virginia 23261-2068.

©1977 Time-Life Books Inc. All rights reserved.
No part of this book may be reproduced in any form or by any
electronic or mechanical means, including information stor-
age and retrieval devices or systems, without prior written
permission from the publisher, except that brief passages may
be quoted for reviews.
Eighth printing. Revised 1985. Printed in U.S.A.
Published simultaneously in Canada.
Library of Congress catalogue card number 76-55869.
School and library distribution by Silver Burdett Company,
Morristown, New Jersey.

TIME-LIFE is a trademark of Time Incorporated U.S.A.

Contents

Metal weather stripping. Bronze weather stripping nailed in the side channels and to the rails of an aging double-hung window plugs the cracks that admit drafts to chill a house in winter and heat it in summer. Not only is this springy metal seal the most effective weather stripping for this type of window, but it is also one of the easiest to fit correctly for an airtight seal (*pages 8 and 9*).

Above all else, a house is built to provide shelter from the elements. To protect the house against invasion by unwanted air and water, heat and cold—even animals and insects—is a principal concern of the homeowner. This battle against the elements is fought with a varied arsenal of materials and equipment. There are plugs and sealers, pumps and vents, insulation, awnings and tinted plastics—plus special techniques and equipment for emergencies such as hurricanes and floods, earthquakes and lightning storms.

Few houses demand every weatherproofing remedy in this book, but sooner or later most require one or more of them to remain sound and comfortable. Every few years, for example, new caulking and perhaps new weather stripping are needed to replace what has worn out and to seal up gaps that appear as the house settles. Once properly sealed, a house may have too little air entering to carry moisture away or to keep the furnace burning efficiently. Therefore, ventilators must be installed that take advantage of natural air currents or that create their own with electric ventilating fans. Intentional ventilation of this sort has a major advantage over the accidental air currents that come through odd cracks and crannies; it lets you control how much air gets in where.

Although ventilation removes airborne moisture, other measures are necessary to cure a house of leaks. More homes than ever have water in the basement. One cause is the proliferation of shopping-center parking lots, which, by reducing natural drainage of rainfall into the earth, send water into residential areas to flood basements that had never been wet before. In some cases, the key to a dry basement may be as simple as cleaning out the gutters or sealing cracks in foundation walls or leaks in the roof. When such routine steps are insufficient, you may have to lay underground pipe to carry water away, perhaps to a dry well, or you may want to apply waterproofing to the foundation, or even install a pump in the basement.

Another kind of seepage has nothing to do with water but exacts a toll in dollars and comfort. In winter, heat escapes from the house through the walls, roof, basement, doors and windows. In summer, heat leaks in by the same routes. Such losses, in either direction, have become intolerably expensive as energy prices have risen—the cost of gas for heating increased about 14 per cent in 4 years in the early Seventies, and the cost of electricity went up almost 25 per cent. Depending on where you live, your house may benefit from as much as a foot of insulation in the attic, for example, and storm windows and doors—a form of insulation you can build as well as install yourself—are a necessity in all but the mildest climates as a finishing touch in making your house impervious to the elements.

Weather Stripping to Block the Drafts

The cracks around doors and windows are the main cause of air leakage in most homes. Weather-stripping cracks can reduce heating and air-conditioning costs as much as 30 per cent.

In many houses, window sashes and doors are grooved to interlock with metal flanges around the frames. If your house lacks this sort of built-in weather stripping, the illustrations on these and the following six pages will show you how to install other types.

There are some simple tests to determine your weather-stripping needs. On a cool, windy day, feel for air leaking in by placing your hand on several places along door and window cracks. Another method is to hold a tissue next to the crack to see if it flutters. Or, shine a flashlight along door and window edges from the outside at night while someone inside watches to see if light penetrates.

Once you know your trouble spots you can select the weather stripping best suited to the job. Materials suitable for both doors and windows come in flexible rolls of metal, felt, plastic foam, rubber or vinyl (below). Types designed for the sides and tops of doors are rigid strips edged with foam, felt or plastic (page 12). Several varieties of door bottoms also can be purchased (page 14).

All come prepackaged with nails or screws, and include enough stripping to cover at least one door or window. Another type fits a channel routed into the door jamb or window frame. It should be installed by a professional.

All weather stripping is installed so the resilient part seals out air by pressing against the door or window. Do not make the seals too tight or windows and doors will not open and close smoothly.

Before beginning, make sure the doors and windows work properly. Doors that do not hang straight may have to be shimmed or sanded to eliminate binding (page 13). Sometimes windows will not shut all the way: the top rail of the lower sash and the bottom rail of the upper sash should meet evenly across the center of the window. If they do not, scrape paint or dirt off top and bottom rails and their channels. It may be necessary to sand the top or bottom of the window.

For double-hung windows, the best easily installed seal is the springy metal stripping shown on these pages. Such strips are nailed only along one edge; the other edge springs out to block leaks. Metal stripping is installed so it cannot be seen when the window is shut.

Felt, rubber and plastic weather stripping (overleaf) are easier to install, but not as long lasting and must be mounted in full view on the sash or frame.

Casement and gliding windows are more difficult to seal and require special solutions (page 11).

A Choice of Materials

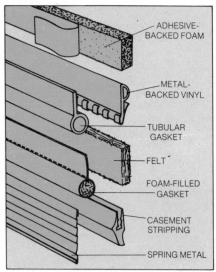

ADHESIVE-BACKED FOAM

METAL-BACKED VINYL

TUBULAR GASKET

FELT

FOAM-FILLED GASKET

CASEMENT STRIPPING

SPRING METAL

Selecting flexible weather stripping. The materials shown above can be used on doors or windows. Durable spring metal is hidden when doors or windows are shut. Metal-backed vinyl or felt is difficult to install, and the vinyl, though applicable to exteriors, may pull away in cold weather or stick when it is warm. Tubular and foam-filled gaskets of vinyl or rubber can be mounted outside. Adhesive-backed foam may come loose on movable surfaces. Felt strips are inexpensive, but they attract dirt, tear easily and must be installed inside. Special vinyl stripping will seal casement windows snugly.

Spring-Metal for Windows

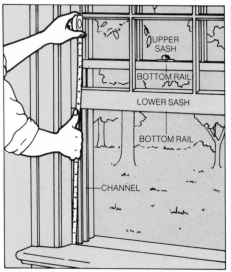

UPPER SASH

BOTTOM RAIL

LOWER SASH

BOTTOM RAIL

CHANNEL

1 Measuring the strips. On double-hung windows, spring-metal weather stripping is installed in the side channels of both upper and lower sashes, on the bottom rails of the upper and lower sashes and on the top rail of the upper sash.

To determine the length of the four side channel strips, raise the lower sash, then measure from the base of one channel to a point 2 inches above the bottom rail of the upper sash. Use tin snips or wire cutters to cut the strips. Finally, measure the bottom rail of the lower sash and cut three strips to this length.

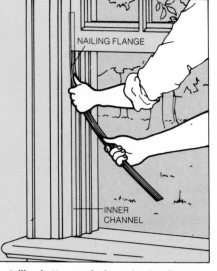

NAILING FLANGE

INNER CHANNEL

2 Installing bottom-sash channel strips. Each metal strip must be installed so the nailing flange lies flush against the inside edge of the frame. Open the lower sash as far as possible and remove any loose paint or dirt from the channels. Slip the end of a strip into the narrow slit between sash and channel, and slide the strip upward until it fills the bottom of the inner channel. Repeat on the other side. If you cannot readily slip the strips into place, scrape out the slits with a thin-bladed knife and try again.

3 **Securing the channel strips.** Fasten the strips by nailing through the holes near the edge. Secure the lower portion of the lower-sash channel strips first; then drop the lower sash and fasten the portion that extends above the top rail.

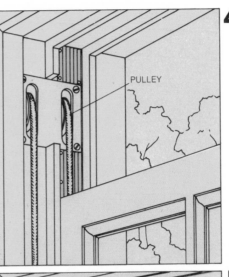

4 **Installing outer-channel strips.** If the window lacks rope or chain pulleys, lower both sashes as far as possible and install the strips in the tops of the outer channels as you did in the bottoms of the inner channels in Steps 2 and 3.

If the window has pulleys, as shown here, proceed as follows. Cut the metal into two pieces —one to fit the space above the pulley and one to extend from the pulley to a point 2 inches below the top rail of the lower sash. Install the short piece above the pulley, and fasten extra tacks across its bottom edge. With the top and bottom sashes still all the way down, carefully pull the rope or chain out of the way and feed the long strip into the outer channel below the pulley. Nail the strip in place, then push both sashes all the way up and fasten the end that protrudes below the upper sash's bottom rail.

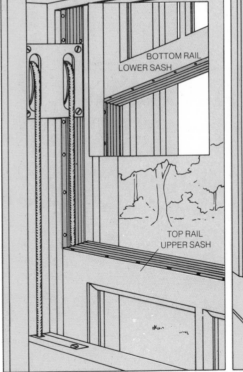

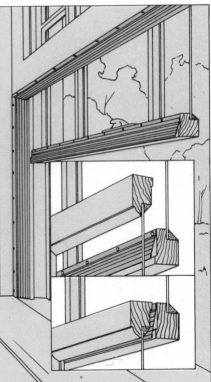

5 **Tightening the seal.** Once the channel strips are nailed in place, use a wide-bladed tool like a putty knife to bend out the unfastened side about ¼ inch, or until the window holds position but does not bind. This increases the spring action and provides a better seal.

6 **Installing top and bottom cross strips.** Metal strips should extend across the full width of the window on the top side of the top rail of the upper sash, and also on the underside of the bottom rail of the bottom sash. The flange to be nailed should be positioned along the inside edge of the window. (Hammer gently or you may crack the glass.) Once in place, pry out the two crosspieces as shown in Step 5.

7 **Mounting the center cross strip.** Install the last metal strip on the inner side of the bottom rail of the upper sash (*above*). The nailing flange should extend across the top edge of the rail. After fastening the strip, sink the nails well into the metal by hammering them again with a nail set or with an inverted flathead nail; this ensures that the sashes will move smoothly yet maintain a tight seal when closed (*inset*). Complete the installation by bending this strip as you have the others.

Using Gaskets and Strips

1 Installing gaskets. While weather-resistant vinyl or rubber gasket strips cannot be hidden away like metal weather stripping, they can be applied to the outside of a window where they are not visible. To ensure a straight, tight seal, maintain tension in the strips while nailing them to the window frame. Their thickened edges should fit snugly against the sides of the sashes. Nail additional strips to the bottom edge of the bottom sash rail and the top edge of the top sash rail, making sure that both gaskets press tightly against the frame when the window is shut.

2 Sealing the meeting rails. Complete the installation of vinyl or rubber gaskets by securing a strip under the bottom rail of the top sash (*below*). Placed against the inside edge, it will seal the crack between the two halves of the window.

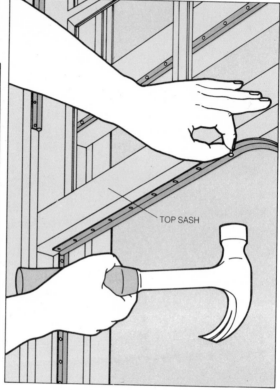

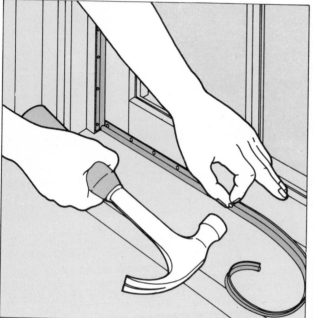

TOP SASH

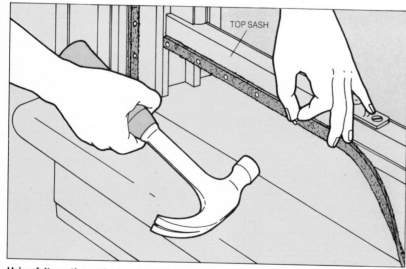

TOP SASH

Using felt weather stripping. Install felt strips as shown for gaskets (*above*), but place the strips on the indoor side of the window sashes and frame. Seal the meeting rails by applying a strip of felt to the interior side of the bottom rail of the upper window sash, positioning the felt as you would spring metal (*page 9, Step 7*).

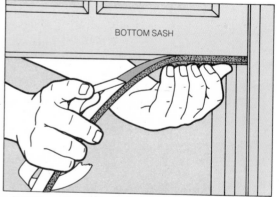

BOTTOM SASH

Installing adhesive-backed stripping. Press the adhesive side of the strip to the clean surface with your fingers as you slowly pull off the protective backing (*above*). Since opening and closing a double-hung window could cause this material to come unstuck from frame edges, use it only on the friction-free areas—the underside of the lower sash's bottom rail and the top side of the upper sash's top rail.

Casement Windows

Weather-stripping metal casements. Metal casement windows can be weatherproofed by a special vinyl gasket with a deep groove that easily slips onto all four edges of the frame. First, apply a vinyl-to-metal adhesive to the frame, then install the vinyl gasket so that the window closes against the flat side of the strips.

Sealing wood casements. Many new styles of wood casements have their own built-in weatherproofing. If yours do not, nail spring metal stripping of the type described on page 8 to the frame. For casements that open outward (*below*), the nailing flange should be placed along the outside edge of the frame. Reverse the position of the nailing flange for windows that open inward.

You can also install felt or adhesive-backed foam stripping on the inside of the frame, but such materials tend to loosen after a few months of frequent opening and closing of the windows.

These same procedures apply to awning-type windows, which are really sidewise casements.

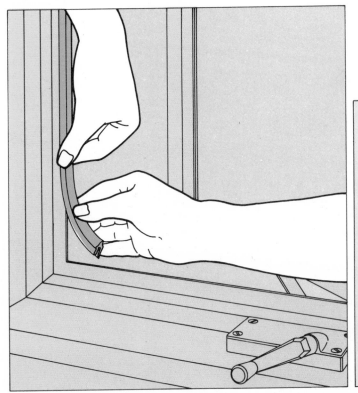

Gliding Windows

Weatherproofing gliding windows. Most new types of wood gliding windows come with weather stripping built in between the frame and the sash. Older types, however, may need sealing. If both sashes move, treat the window as if it were a double-hung window turned on its side.

For windows with one gliding sash, treat only the movable part. Install a strip of spring metal in the side channel that receives the movable sash, lining up the nailing flange along the inside edge. Then nail vinyl or rubber gasket along the exterior top, bottom and outer edges of the gliding sash. The outer strip will fit snugly against the rail of the inside sash where the window sections meet.

Most metal gliding windows have rubber weather stripping in the tracks of each sash but, like wood gliders, should be sealed where the sashes meet. Attach the gasket with vinyl-to-metal adhesive.

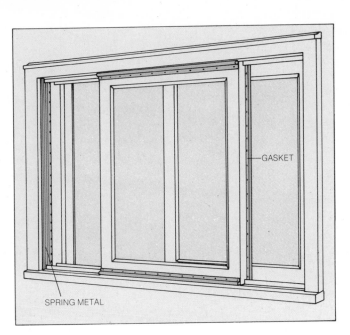

GASKET

SPRING METAL

Weather-stripping Doors

The big leaks in most houses are around doors. They lack the twofold edge enclosures of double-hung windows, so an open crack is inevitable. Any of various types of weather stripping can fill the crack, but it cannot do so effectively unless the door fits properly. If weather stripping is attached to a binding door, it may make the door impossible to open or close. So the first step in weatherproofing a door is to adjust hinges, and sand or plane edges until it opens and closes smoothly, leaving a narrow, uniform space between edge and jamb.

Generally you can see how the door fits by looking at the edges all around. To find invisible binds, slide thin cardboard between the closed door and the jamb, or rub colored chalk on the door edge—it will rub off on the jamb at binds.

Most often a door sticks because loosened hinge screws made it sag. Tighten the screws. If the screws will not hold, replace them with longer ones or stuff the screw holes with toothpicks. If screw-tightening does not solve the problem, try shifting the door by spacing hinge leaves with thin material (*opposite, top*) or plane off the door edge at the binds. If the entire latch side binds, remove the door and plane the hinge side—so you will not have to move the lock—then reset the hinges.

Once you have fixed the door so it operates smoothly, one of the weather-stripping materials illustrated below will stop up the cracks at the sides and top. The crack at the bottom of the door is sealed differently, with any of several devices described overleaf. For sliding doors, follow the instructions given for gliding windows *(page 11)*.

Types of weather stripping. Most durable and effective of weather strippings intended for do-it-yourself installation is the so-called V-strip. A doubled-over strip of springy metal, it fits between door edge and jamb, filling the crack. Other types attach to the doorframe—or the doorstop molding—so that their flexible edges press against the door face when it is closed. Some are rolls of felt or plastic foam backed with adhesive so that they can be stuck on. Sturdier and less obtrusive are wood, metal or plastic strips, edged with plastic tubing or foam, that look like extra decorative trim on the doorstop.

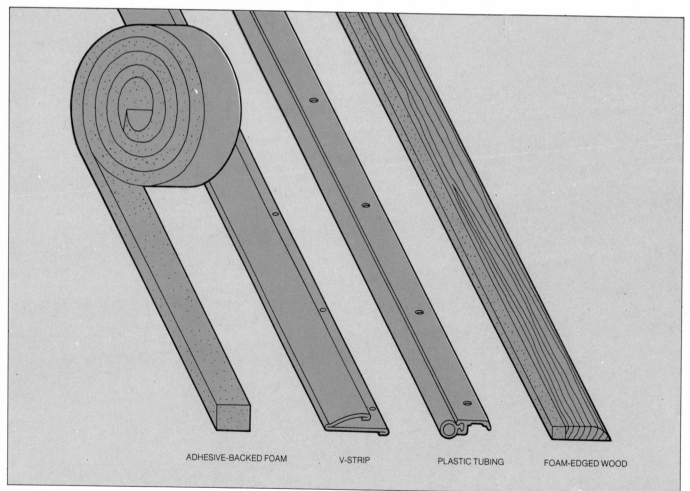

ADHESIVE-BACKED FOAM   V-STRIP   PLASTIC TUBING   FOAM-EDGED WOOD

Straightening a door. If the bind is on the top or bottom edge of the door, plane or sand wood from that edge until the door fits easily. If a door binds on its leading edge—where the lock is installed—it is not necessary to remove any wood. Instead, insert a shim—a piece cut from a plastic bottle—under the jamb leaf of one hinge. Open the door, put a piece of wood under the bottom for support, unscrew the leaf and add shims until binding is eliminated. For binds near the top of the leading edge, shim out the lower hinge; shim out the upper hinge for lower binds. For binds on the hinge side, shim the hinge nearest the bind.

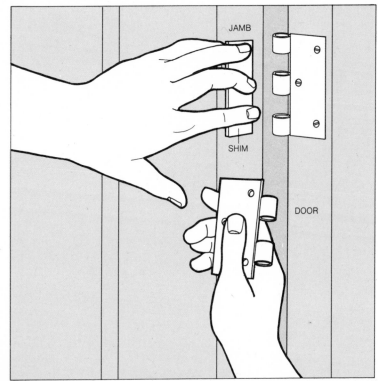

Installing V-strip weather stripping. Cut strips to run along both sides and the top of the door, trimming away sections that would cover hinges and the lock. With the nailing flange against the doorstop and the point of the V facing the door, nail each strip to the jamb.

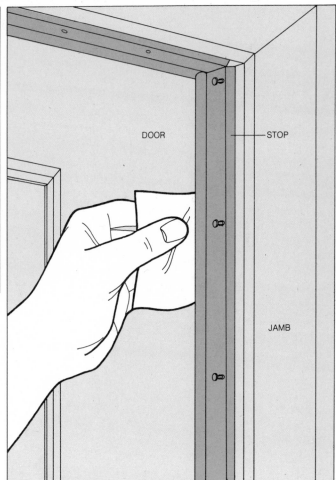

Attaching doorstop weather stripping. Cut the strips to the lengths of the top and side doorstop moldings. With the door closed, position the top piece against the top stop, pressing the flexible edge lightly against the door face. Attach the strip to the stop with nails or screws but do not drive the fasteners all the way. Install the side strips the same way. Test the positioning by sliding a piece of paper between the door and the flexible edge; it should barely slide all around. Do not position too tightly or the door will not close. Adjust strip positions, resetting fasteners as necessary, then drive the fasteners all the way.

Seals for the Bottom

Door bottoms. A number of devices are made to plug the most troublesome door crack, that at the bottom. Those called sweeps drag a flexible strip against thresholds; special thresholds press flexible material upward against the bottom edge. All come in many shapes and sizes, and most adjust to fit any door. Plain sweeps (*top, far right*) attach to the bottom outside edge of the door; one has a spring to raise it as the door opens and lower it when the door is shut. Bottom sweeps of the type shown at bottom, near right, slide onto the underside of doors. Like the plain sweeps, bottom sweeps can be installed without removing the door. Threshold weather strip fastens to the sill, replacing the existing threshold. For overhead garage doors, plastic or rubber stripping adds a flexible bottom edge.

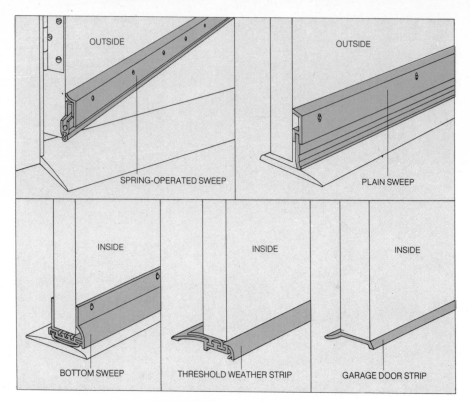

OUTSIDE

OUTSIDE

SPRING-OPERATED SWEEP

PLAIN SWEEP

INSIDE

INSIDE

INSIDE

BOTTOM SWEEP

THRESHOLD WEATHER STRIP

GARAGE DOOR STRIP

Installing Sweeps

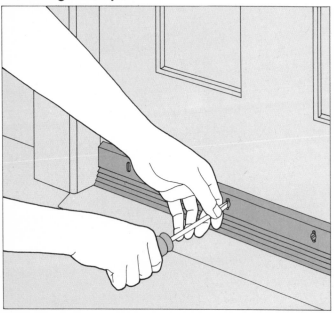

Attaching a plain door sweep. Cut the sweep to door width and screw it across the bottom edge on the outdoor side so it fits snugly against the threshold when the door is shut, yet allows the door to open and close smoothly. Most sweeps have slots, so positioning is easily adjusted.

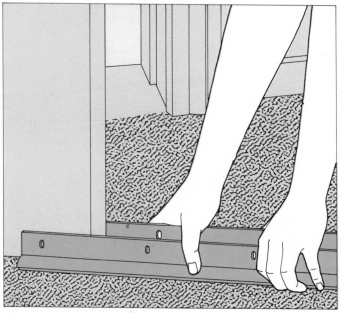

Attaching a bottom sweep. Adjust the width of the sweep to the thickness of your door by slipping the movable piece into the appropriate groove on the channel base. Cut the sweep to the width of the door. Then swing the door open and slide the sweep under the bottom of the door. Close the door, let the sweep drop against the threshold, then drive the attachment screws in their slots partway. Adjust positioning until the sweep drop is snug, but not so tight that the door will not work smoothly. Tighten the screws.

Installing Weatherproof Thresholds

1 **Removing the existing threshold.** Shield the floor or carpet around the door with pieces of cardboard secured by masking tape. Try to remove the threshold with a pry bar. If it does not lift up easily, cut through at each end with a backsaw (*below*) and force up the center piece.

2 **Knocking out end pieces.** If the new threshold is the same height as the old one, tap out the ends with a mallet and chisel as shown below. Otherwise, saw through the door stops to heighten the opening and release the end pieces as well. Clean the sill with turpentine.

3 **Installing the new threshold.** Cut the threshold to fit tightly against both sides of the door jamb. Position the threshold so that the flap side of the plastic seal is toward the outdoors. Lift up the plastic flap and insert screws through the holes in the strip underneath.

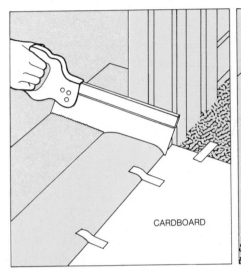

CARDBOARD

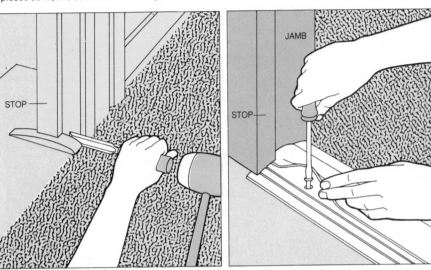

STOP

JAMB

STOP

Strips for Garage Doors

Sealing wood overhead doors. Paint the garage door bottom to protect it against moisture. Then cut stripping of thick rubber or plastic to length with wire cutters. Pull the door partway down so the bottom edge is accessible. Brace the door against a 2-by-4 and fasten the weather stripping with heavy nails so that the thickened edge of the channel is on the outside of the door. The material has enough resiliency to adjust for a tight seal against uneven concrete floors.

2-BY-4

Plugging Up All the Cracks and Crannies

Houses are built of a number of different materials working together to keep out drafts, dust, moisture and insects. Because these varied materials expand and contract at different rates with changing temperatures, cracks and gaps are bound to appear wherever two different materials meet. Traffic vibrations, the closing and opening of windows and doors, even the pressure of wind against the roof and walls widen these openings. If you add together all these unintentional vents in an average house—around the windows and doors, at the spots where pipes and wires enter the house, and in a surprising variety of other places *(drawing, opposite, top)*—the total space would equal a hole 2 feet square.

You can choose among dozens of sealant materials to caulk these gaps. All are air- and watertight. Almost all come in at least two consistencies: gun grade, sold in cartridges that fit a caulking gun *(page 18)*, and used for cracks no wider than a pencil; and knife grade, applied to wider cracks with a caulking or putty knife. For very thin cracks, you may prefer caulking that comes in a handy tube; for very wide ones, such as the gaps around storm windows and air conditioners, you may want to use cord or rope caulking, which comes in rolls and is easily pressed in with the fingers. Whatever sealant you use should be applied to clean, dry surfaces on a warm, dry day.

Far more important than these comparatively minor differences of consistency or packaging, however, is the chemical composition of the sealant you choose. Depending on its composition, the federal government has assigned every sealant to one of three performance groups, shown in the chart below.

At the lowest level, in the basic group, are ropes, cords and sealants based on natural oils and resins. The intermediate group, consisting mainly of natural or synthetic rubbers, sticks better to most building materials and is elastic enough to accommodate moderate changes in the width or depth of a crack. Newly developed synthetic materials make up the high-performance group—the most expensive of the three, but in many cases well worth the extra cost. These are the most versatile of all sealants, the easiest to apply as well as the most durable—in one case, the silicones, so durable and so new that the working life of a caulk has yet to be determined.

A Sealant for Every Surface

	Special uses	Sealant	Durability (years)	Adhesion	Shrinkage resistance
Basic performance	glazing	oil and resin caulks	1 to 7	fair to good	poor
	very wide gaps	polybutane cord or rope	1 to 2	none	excellent
Intermediate performance	indoor and protected surfaces	nonacrylic latex; PVA	2 to 10	good, except to metal	fair
	indoor and protected surfaces	acrylic latex	2 to 10	excellent, except to metal	fair
	metal-to-masonry	butyl rubber	7 to 10	excellent	fair
	anywhere	chlorosulfonated polyethylene	15 to 20	good	good
	concrete	neoprene	15 to 20	excellent	good
High performance	anywhere	polysulfide	20	excellent	excellent
	anywhere	polyurethane	20	excellent	excellent
	anywhere	silicone	20 or more	good, excellent with primer	excellent

Finding gaps and cracks. The house at left is marked in orange at the points where caulking is generally needed. If your chimney rises along an outside wall, caulk the line at which it meets the siding. One trouble spot is not shown in the drawing: the point at which a pipe or wire enters from an unheated attic, basement or crawl space; always caulk that entry point.

Judging a sealant. All the sealants in this chart are general-purpose caulks for wood, masonry, metal and glass, but many have areas of special usefulness, listed in the first column. Use the other columns to match a specific sealant to your needs. Manufacturers' trade names rarely indicate the composition of a sealant or of a cleaner to use at the end of a job—read the fine print on the label to find the generic names shown here.

Adhesion is a measure of a sealant's ability to bond to a surface; shrinkage resistance measures its ability to stay there under changing conditions. A sealant is tack-free when it loses its initial stickiness; in the curing stage, it hardens and dries to its final form. For sealants that need primers, follow the manufacturer's instructions.

Tack-free (hours)	Cure (days)	Cleaner	Primer	Paint	
2 to 24	up to 1 year	paint thinner	needed on porous surfaces	should be painted	lowest cost; may stain unprimed surface
remains moist and pliant		no cleaning required	none needed	should not be painted	often used for temporary or seasonal caulks
¼ to ½	3	water	none needed	optional	deteriorates in sunlight; paint outdoor caulks
¼ to ½	3	water	needed on porous surfaces	optional	easy to apply in cool weather and on relatively damp surfaces
½ to 1½	7	naphtha, paint thinner	none needed	optional	high moisture resistance; relatively difficult to make into a neat bead
24 to 48	60 to 90	toluene, xylene	none needed	optional	relatively easy to apply
1	30 to 60	toluene, xylene, MEK	none needed	optional	toxic; apply only when ample ventilation can be provided
24 to 72	7	toluene, TCE, MEK	neoprene primer needed	optional	nontoxic when cured, but may irritate skin when it is being applied
24	4 to 14	acetone, MEK, paint thinner	none needed	optional	relatively easy to apply; nontoxic when cured
1	2 to 5	naphtha, tolnol, xylol paint thinner	follow manufacturer's instructions	follow manufacturer's instructions	high moisture resistance; can be applied at low temperatures; nontoxic when cured

Five Ways to Seal Cracks

Most of the newer and more efficient sealants are usually applied with a caulking gun. The most popular type uses individual cartridges *(top right)* that are thrown away when empty. Getting a smooth flow of sealant—a proper bead —may require practice. So if you are doing the job for the first time, make a few trial strokes.

While a caulking gun is best for most jobs, some small repairs are more conveniently done in other ways *(opposite)*: caulks that are squeezed like toothpaste from a collapsible tube, glazing compound that is pressed into cracks with your fingers, ropelike strands that are pushed into place and filler that must be tamped into openings. Whatever you use, thoroughly clean the area around a crack, removing old sealant and chipped paint with a wood chisel or putty knife. Wipe the crack with turpentine, then use a stiff brush to get rid of remaining dirt. Do not try to caulk when temperatures are below 50° F.—the sealant will be too hard to handle easily and it will not stick to the cold surfaces.

Using a caulking gun. Hold the gun at a 45° angle to the surface and squeeze the trigger with a steady pressure. Keep the gun slightly slanted in the direction you are moving and draw it along slowly so that the sealant not only fills the crack but also overlaps the edges.

To get a smooth bead, fill a single seam in one stroke if you can. Pressure inside the cartridge will keep pushing out the sealant after you release the trigger; to avoid getting a lumpy bead, where several strokes are necessary release the trigger quickly at the end of each stroke and continue to move the gun as you slowly squeeze the trigger for the next stroke. When you want to stop the flow of sealant altogether, disengage the trigger by turning the plunger so that the teeth point upward and then pull the rod back an inch or so.

The Versatile Caulking Gun

Caulking manufacturers package their products in standard cartridges that fit interchangeably into a caulking gun. The gun pushes caulking out of the cartridge with a trigger-activated plunger. To load a caulking gun, turn the plunger rod so that the teeth face up and pull it back as far as you can. Insert the cartridge in the top opening and press the nozzle firmly into the slot at the front end. Turn the plunger rod so that the teeth face down and engage the trigger mechanism. After loading the cartridge, snip off the sealed tip of its nozzle at a 45° angle. The nozzle is tapered so you can make an opening for a thin, medium or heavy bead. Next, insert a nail through the tip to puncture the seal at the base of the nozzle. After use, plug the nozzle with the nail.

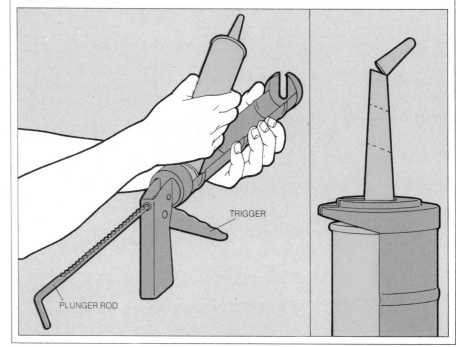

TRIGGER

PLUNGER ROD

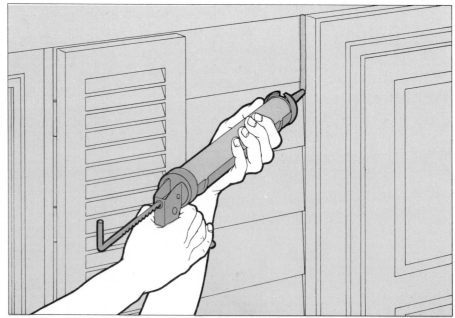

Using a roll-up tube. For sealing around outside water faucets (*below*), vents and other small areas, use a squeeze tube. Snip the tip off the nozzle in the same way as for a gun cartridge (*opposite, top right*) to give a bead of the desired size. Apply the sealant by squeezing the tube from the bottom—much as you would a toothpaste tube—and draw it slowly across the crack.

Sealing with glazing compound. To keep cold air from leaking around the joint between glass windowpanes and their frames, press this soft, sticky material along the edge of the glass with your fingers. Then smooth it with a putty knife. Turpentine can be used with the knife in order to make a smoother finish and it can also be used with a rag to clean off excess compound.

Applying ropelike caulk. This material, especially useful for temporary seals and hard-to-reach corners, can be unrolled in single or multiple strands, depending on the size of the crack. Press it in with your fingers—wetting them will make them less likely to stick to the sealant.

Sealing large cracks. For a crack more than ½ inch deep—common at the joint between siding and foundations (*above*)—first plug the crack with sponge rubber or oakum. The latter is durable but very oily. Push the filler into a crack with a screwdriver or putty knife. Then apply one or more beads of sealant with a caulking gun.

2

The Battle against Moisture

A splash block to keep a basement dry. The solution to basement dampness is often simple and inexpensive. If your downspouts discharge rainwater and melting snow directly onto the soil around the foundation, that water may be reappearing as seepage on basement walls or as puddles on the floor. Installing a masonry splash block *(left)* under the downspout and tilting it to channel water away from the house will often cure the dampness for only the cost of the block.

Anyone who has coped with rain-soaked plaster and flooded basements can be forgiven skepticism when a professional roofer speaks of hundred-year-old roofs that, although they leaked daylight in a dozen places, let in hardly a drop during a rainstorm. The story is not an exaggeration. Many older roofs are covered with wood shingles, which have the happy faculty of plugging their own small leaks. The wood expands as it absorbs the initial rainfall, effectively sealing small holes. Unfortunately, the leaks and moisture problems encountered by modern homeowners go beyond small holes and are rarely self-correcting; prompt action must be taken before water causes serious and expensive harm.

In addition to such obvious effects as puddles and peeling paint, water can cause damage more slowly and in less noticeable areas. An ice dam on the roof *(page 50)* often hides water seeping under shingles. The swelling and shrinking caused by changes in moisture levels makes wood joists and beams warp and bow. Damp timbers are susceptible to the fungi that cause mold, mildew and dry rot —which can reduce sturdy beams to dry powder; damp wood near the foundation also invites termite infestations *(pages 96F-96G)*.

Keeping the house dry is a twofold task. On the outside, water must be channeled off the house and away from the foundation. Inside, water vapor—moisture that is not in liquid form but is in the air as humidity—must be carefully controlled. Some water vapor enters the house with humid outdoor air, but enormous amounts are generated inside the home by bathing, cooking and laundering.

Problems caused by condensed moisture can be cured by improving the ventilation in your home. By installing strategically placed openings in the attic and basement, you can ensure a constant movement of air that will push warm moisture outdoors, taking advantage of the natural tendency of hot air to rise *(pages 52-58)*. In problem areas—kitchens, bathrooms and laundries—ducting and electric fans may be needed. An electric dehumidifier can also help.

Leaks and seepage originating outdoors can often be corrected by such simple measures as redirecting the flow from downspouts *(opposite)* and banking the earth around the foundation. If the basement still leaks, try waterproofing the porous masonry from the inside with the appropriate paint, sealant or cement *(pages 30-33)*. More serious drainage problems, or a rising ground-water level under the basement, will require digging a dry well or excavating around the foundation to install drain tile and waterproof the exterior walls. When even these measures fail to keep water out of the basement, an electric sump pump provides the last line of defense, discharging the water as fast as it enters.

21

Channeling Water Away from Your House

Water that collects around the foundation of a house can exert tremendous pressure—as much as 500 pounds per square foot—eventually causing structural damage and wet basements. Channeling rain and melting snow away from the foundation is thus a primary concern of every homeowner.

You can protect a house located on sloping ground by digging a system of swales—drainage ditches that are planted over with grass and are so shallow they are almost unnoticeable—to collect most of the runoff and reroute it away from the foundation (opposite). Rain that falls within this defensive line can be deflected by banking earth near the house to form a sloping watershed. If the dirt would cover part of a basement window, install a window well (below). Do not pile dirt closer than 8 inches to wood siding, however, or insects will use the

embankment as a bridge into the house.

Areas directly below eaves must be protected from water coursing off the roof; raindrops can erode soil and expose the foundation. Gutters and downspouts are the common means by which this water is carried away. But these conduits are not the only solutions; indeed, they have drawbacks that the homeowner should keep in mind. They need maintenance—painting, patching, repositioning—and replacement when they wear out. They get clogged with debris. In northern climates they become blocked with snow and ice, causing buildups on the gutters and the roof itself.

Use gutters and downspouts where they are essential, but let rain fall freely off the roof if the ground below will bear it. A steep embankment often is protection enough. Thin strips of gravel, walks and patios are better still. And dense

shrubbery planted under the eaves not only impedes erosion but adds a note of grace to your landscaping. Be careful, though, to avoid greenery with large root systems; the roots may grow against the foundation and crack it.

Wherever downspouts are used, the area around them must be given extra protection from the heavy concentration of water they spew forth. If the ground slopes sharply, you may need to install only a splash block that will absorb the impact and disperse the torrent. But if the house is on level ground you probably will need a downspout extension. This may be as simple as a coiled plastic pipe that unfurls under the force of running water, or it may involve underground piping and, in extreme cases, a dry well (pages 26-29). Again, be guided by the rule that the best system is the simplest one that will get the job done.

Installing a window well. The cavity around a basement window that extends below ground level exposes the foundation to serious water damage unless proper drainage is provided. The solution is a window well. The liner of an inexpensive and easy-to-install well consists of a ready-made, oval-shaped sheet of galvanized steel, usually corrugated. Available at building-supply stores, the sheets come in a variety of sizes that will fit around almost any window.

Buy a liner 6 inches wider than the window. Dig a hole for the liner 1 foot deeper than the bottom of the window. Center the liner in the bottom of the hole (right). Spread 4 inches of gravel on the bottom of the well, both inside and outside the liner, then fill the rest of the hole behind the liner —away from the house—with earth. Plant sod or place a thin strip of gravel on top of the earth so that rain falling around the perimeter of the well will drain away naturally.

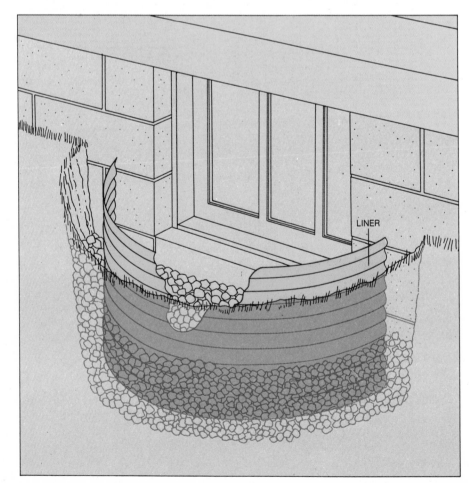

LINER

A System of Swales and Berms

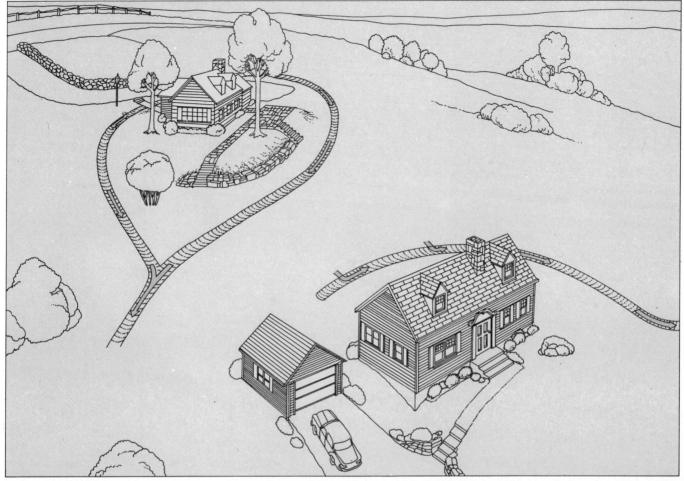

Laying out drainage ditches. Plan ditches —swales—across the slope above your house to intercept water coming downhill, making them long enough to divert the water around the foundation. The downhill house in this picture requires only a single curved ditch to keep the basement dry. The uphill house needs a more elaborate system of connecting ditches to direct water away from its downhill neighbor.

Digging a drainage ditch. Make your ditches 2 to 3 feet wide and 6 to 10 inches deep. As you dig, pile the dirt on the downhill side of the ditch to make a lip—a berm—to help trap water in the ditch. Next, spread 2 or 3 inches of gravel in the ditch, then fill it the rest of the way with topsoil, leaving the downhill lip. Place sod over the lip and plant long-rooted grass such as Bermuda in the ditch to hold the topsoil and gravel in place.

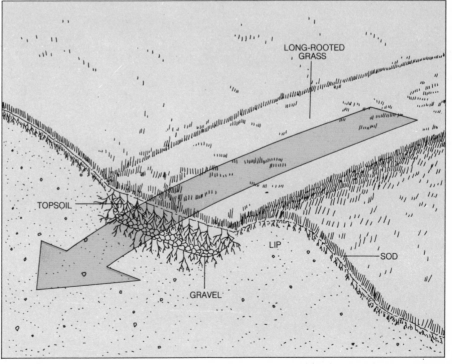

LONG-ROOTED GRASS

TOPSOIL

LIP

SOD

GRAVEL

How to Make Gutters Work

When gutters are clogged at blocked downspouts, rain water, left to find its own way, will pour off the eaves and settle into the ground below, and may then seep into the house. Gutters and downspouts need at least semiannual inspection, especially in regions that receive large snowfalls. The weight of snow and ice can force a gutter out of alignment or break it away from its supports. And, while many gutters today are made of weather-resistant aluminum and plastic, some are wood or steel, and these require inspection for rot or corrosion.

When you are inspecting a gutter, you may need a ladder stabilizer to keep the ladder's weight off the gutter. Debris in gutters, on screens or downspouts not only slows the water flow, but speeds corrosion. Clear the downspout cage, gutters and gutter screens, if used.

To give momentum to the flowing water, gutters must be canted toward their downspouts. A telltale discoloration will mark any section where the gutter sags and retains a pool of water. Such sags can be mended as shown (bottom right).

While up on the ladder, also inspect for peeling paint, rusted areas, loose hangers or joints, and split downspouts. Small patches of rust can be scraped clean with a wire brush, then coated with gutter cement or an asphalt-aluminum paint. Areas that have rusted badly can be patched with gutter cement and light-gauge aluminum or the defective runs can be replaced (opposite). New runs of gutters can be ordered from manufacturers or building-supply stores.

A downspout cage. To prevent downspouts from clogging with leaves and debris, install a wire cage or strainer (below). The strainer will trap leaves while permitting water to flow down the spout. Periodically inspect the gutter; unless collected debris is cleaned away from the cage it will mat and impede the water flow.

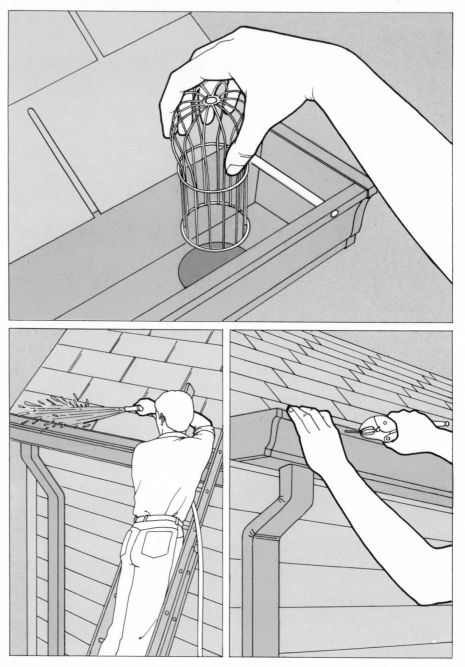

Detecting misalignment. To determine when a gutter is bent out of alignment, spray water on the roof with a garden hose (above). Then watch the flow of water along the gutter; it will pool in the low spots that need alignment.

Realigning gutters. If the gutter is supported by nails, use locking-grip pliers to twist them out (above); hammer claws would damage the rim of the gutter. Reposition the nails or gutter hangers to return the gutter to the proper alignment.

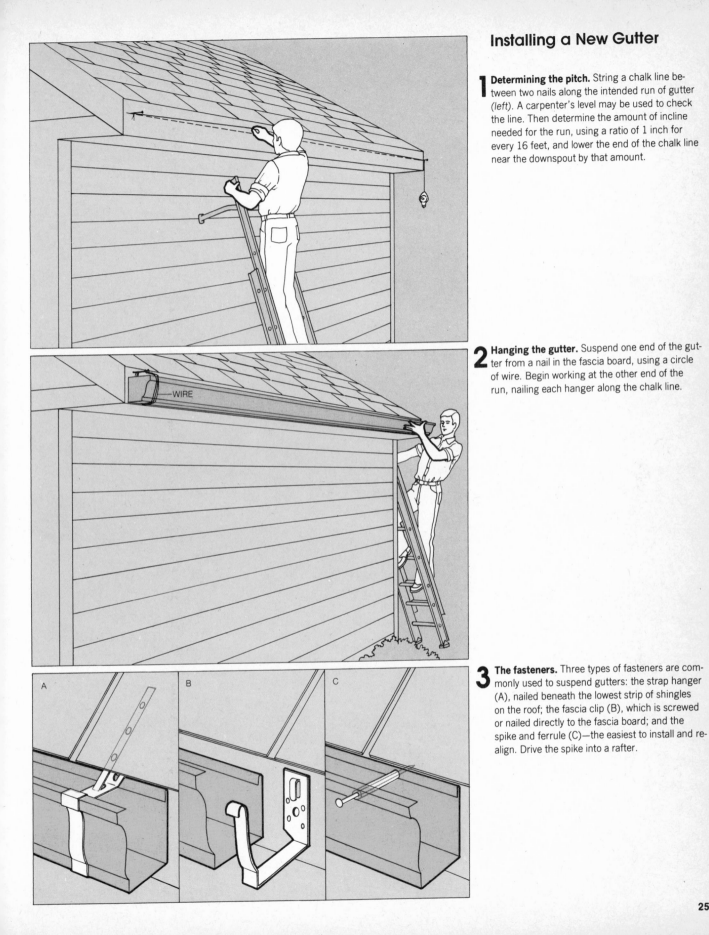

Installing a New Gutter

1 Determining the pitch. String a chalk line between two nails along the intended run of gutter (*left*). A carpenter's level may be used to check the line. Then determine the amount of incline needed for the run, using a ratio of 1 inch for every 16 feet, and lower the end of the chalk line near the downspout by that amount.

WIRE

2 Hanging the gutter. Suspend one end of the gutter from a nail in the fascia board, using a circle of wire. Begin working at the other end of the run, nailing each hanger along the chalk line.

A   B   C

3 The fasteners. Three types of fasteners are commonly used to suspend gutters: the strap hanger (A), nailed beneath the lowest strip of shingles on the roof; the fascia clip (B), which is screwed or nailed directly to the fascia board; and the spike and ferrule (C)—the easiest to install and realign. Drive the spike into a rafter.

Laying Drains Underground

Even the most careful gutter maintenance and repair may leave you vulnerable to basement flooding if your downspouts discharge water directly upon the loose earth near the foundation of a house. Downspouts should drain onto paved areas whenever possible. You can buy ready-made extensions that attach to the end of a downspout and lead to a nearby paved patio or driveway. If no paved area is near the downspout, a splash block made of cement, tile, brick or even plastic and extending 2 or 3 feet from the side of the house will reduce the erosion caused by the water pouring from a downspout. Another alternative is a perforated plastic hose attached to the end of the spout. It unrolls when it is full and squirts water out evenly along its length.

By far the most effective method of conveying gutter water away from the foundation, however, is through buried pipe—generally referred to as tile—3 to 4 inches in diameter, which is attached below ground to an extension of the downspout. Tile traditionally is made of terra cotta, but an improved plastic variety is available for a comparable price. Plastic tile is unbreakable and, because it bends, requires no special pieces for making joints, as does clay pipe.

Tile leading away from the house can extend underground to a storm sewer or culvert if either is nearby, or to a dry well *(overleaf)*. A perforated type of plastic tile *(shown on these pages)* does not need an outlet; it allows water to seep into the ground along its length in much the same way as the aboveground downspout hose does.

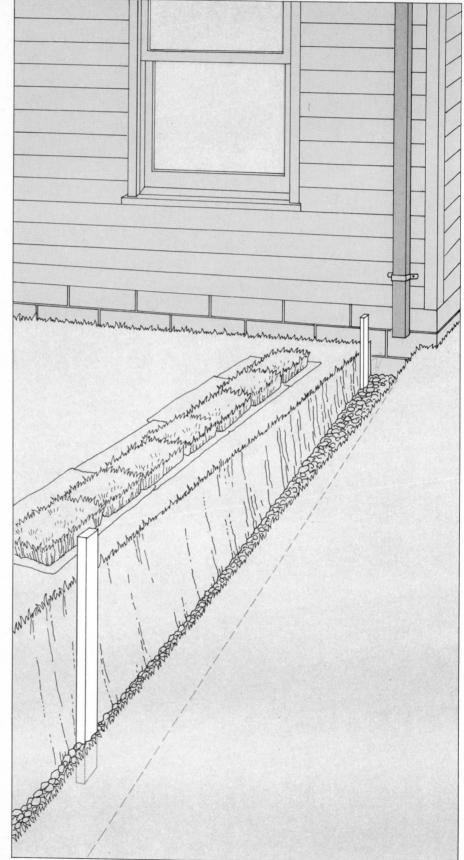

1 **Digging the ditch.** Measure a 12-foot stretch from the downspout at a right angle to the side of the house and mark each end with a stake. Remove foot-wide patches of sod between the stakes and lay them, grass side up, by the ditch. Using a pointed shovel, dig a ditch that slopes from 12 inches below the ground next to the house to a depth of 24 inches at the far end. Line the ditch with 2 to 4 inches of gravel.

2 Installing the tile. Lay a 12-foot length of perforated plastic tile 4 inches in diameter along the
ditch. Slip the end of the tile nearest the house
into a piece of bell-shaped, terra-cotta tile slightly
larger in diameter than the plastic tile. Slide the
terra-cotta tile into place so it collars the downspout. Prop up the assembly with bricks. Line the
crack between the spout and the bell edges with
cloth or paper; fill the bell with cement.

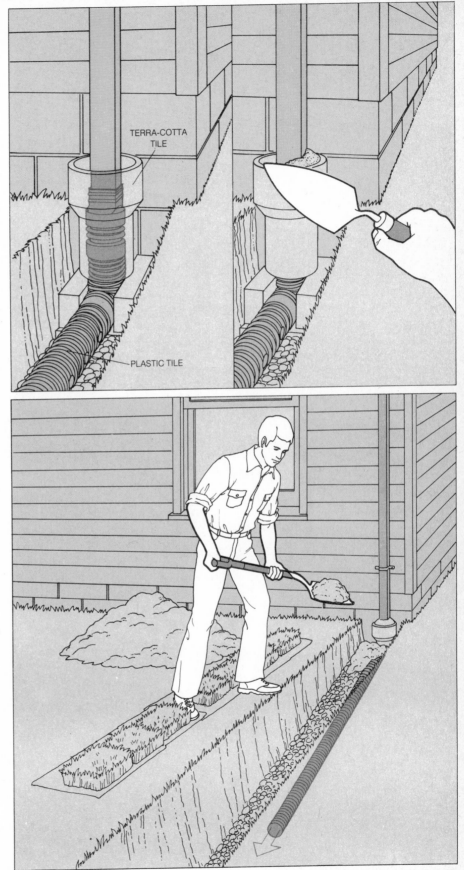

TERRA-COTTA
TILE

PLASTIC TILE

3 Backfilling the ditch. Bury the plastic tile under
2 to 4 inches of gravel. Then, starting at the
end nearest the house, backfill the ditch. Lay the
sod back in place and gently tamp each piece
down with your foot. The slight mound that is cre-
ated by the tile will settle in time.

Building a Dry Well

In densely populated areas where town ordinances often forbid draining rain water into the street or sewer, another method for dispersing runoff is through a dry well—a pit that collects water and lets it slowly percolate into the soil. However, in some localities even dry wells are prohibited, because they may disturb nearby septic systems. Before building one, check the local health department rules or building codes.

Some dry wells are huge, cement-lined bunkers best left for a contractor to build. But a do-it-yourself type can easily be made from a standard 55-gallon oil drum available from service stations or farm-supply outlets at a nominal cost. Prepare the drum by removing top and bottom and cutting a hole in its side with a cold chisel as shown at right. Then choose a place for the well at least 10 feet from the downspout and along the track of the underground drain tile that will connect to the drum.

Excavating a hole 5 feet deep may be difficult in rocky soil. If a pick or breaker bar are not adequate for breaking large rocks in the hole, use a sledgehammer.

1 **Cutting the drum.** Use a ¾-inch cold chisel to remove the top and bottom of the drum and to carve a hole in its side large enough to admit drain tile that is 4 inches in diameter. First knock the chisel through the metal with a ball-peen hammer. Then use the carving edge of the chisel to slice sideways through the drum. Wear gloves and always cut from the outside of the drum. After cutting the tile hole, use a chisel and hammer to punch about 25 small drain holes spaced uniformly all around the drum.

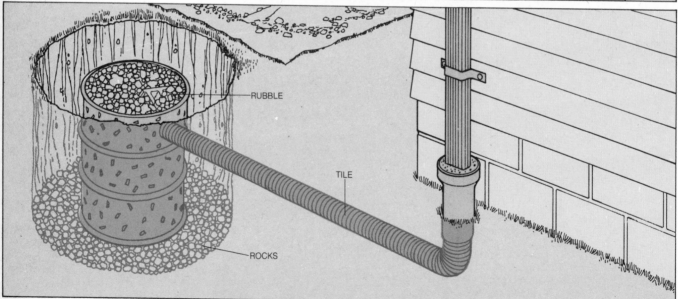

RUBBLE

TILE

ROCKS

2 **Placing the drum.** Remove and save the sod from an area 6 feet in diameter. Dig the hole to a 5-foot depth. Line the bottom with 2 to 4 inches of small rocks, and sink the barrel into place.

Connect the underground drain tile to the drum through the hole. (The method for installing tile is shown on pages 26-27.) Fill the drum with miscellaneous masonry rubble or large rocks.

3 Wrapping with mesh. Use a 10-foot-long, 4-foot-wide section of ¼-inch wire mesh to circle the drum. Using tin snips, cut a 4-inch-wide opening 6 inches into one end of the mesh at the level that the tile enters the drum. At the other end of the mesh, twist on several short pieces of scrap wire for holding the ends of the mesh together. Slide the mesh around the drum, fitting the opening around the tile, overlapping the ends and tying them together with the pieces of short wire.

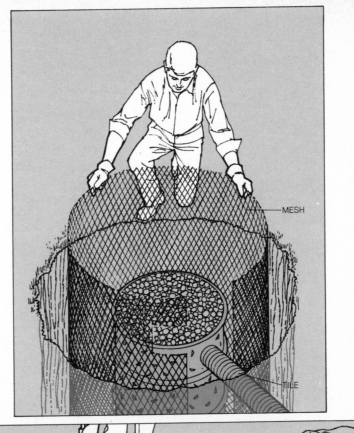

MESH

TILE

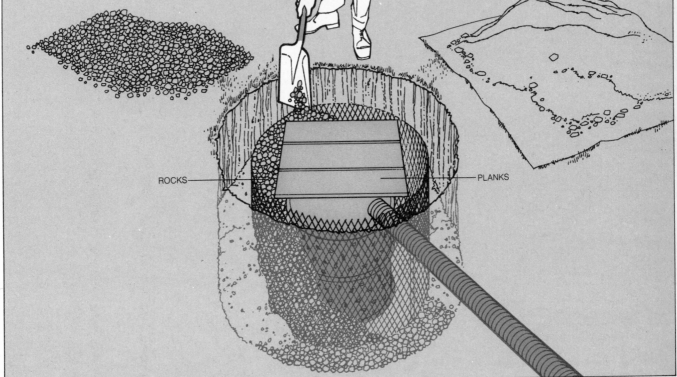

ROCKS

PLANKS

4 Filling the well. Cover the top of the drum with ¼-inch wire mesh and sturdy planks to prevent earth or surface water from entering. Fill the hole, alternately putting small rocks between the mesh and drum, and soil between the mesh and the sides of the well. Filling the gravel first would cause the mesh to open. Cover the drum with at least 1 foot of soil and replace the sod.

Choosing the Right Remedy for a Wet Basement

The causes of a wet basement generally lie outside it, but even the best landscaping and gutter system *(pages 22-25)* may not solve the problem, and often cracks or holes in basement walls admit water that otherwise would stay outside. Much wetness can be eliminated by fixing interior walls, but work on the exterior may be necessary.

If the basement is damp but not wet —you see no patches of water but feel excess humidity or see its effects in mildew —the steps are fairly simple. Dampness may arise from water vapor generated by appliances in the house such as dish- and clothes washers—clothes driers are the worst offenders and their exhausts should be vented outdoors *(pages 66-67)*.

Seepage through walls or floor may introduce water as well as humidity, and sometimes humid air generated inside the house may condense into liquid on masonry surfaces, suggesting that moisture is entering from outdoors. To determine whether the problem is inside or outside—and whether ventilation is a sufficient solution—perform the following test. Tape a 16-inch square of heavy plastic sheeting to the wall below ground level. Remove it after several days: dampness underneath means that water is seeping into the basement between grains of sand and cement in a wall that looks solid. If the plastic-covered area is dry and the wall around it is damp, then water is condensing from moist air that is inside the basement.

If seepage is the problem, you may be able to block it with a coat of waterproof cement paint or, if necessary, layers of patching mortar over masonry interior walls and floor. A dirt floor is a common source of seepage; if you have one, cover it. Polyethylene plastic will do if you need not use the basement; if you must walk on the floor, lay sturdier covering —concrete or, at the least, roll roofing.

Cracks are more serious than seepage or condensation. They can be caused by settling, infiltrating tree roots, water pressure against walls or floor, or even by minor earthquake tremors.

You may first notice a crack on a rainy day as water streams into the basement. The flood can be stopped and the crack fixed by channeling water out through a short hose, then plugging the leak with hydraulic cement, which hardens on contact with water *(page 33)*.

Once the crisis has passed—or if you discover the crack before it floods the basement—check to determine whether it is a moving crack or a stationary one, since each type calls for a different remedy. Mark the wall or floor on each side of the crack and carefully measure the distance between the marks. Remeasure the distance after two weeks. If it is unchanged, the crack is stationary. A change in the space between the marks indicates a moving crack. Try repairing stationary cracks from the inside of the basement first *(opposite)*. If such a patch proves ineffective by itself, the crack probably extends through the wall and you must seal the outside of the foundation too. A concrete patch will work for most cracks, but if the exterior wall of the foundation is badly damaged, you may have to excavate, patch and seal a large section of the wall *(page 36)*.

Moving cracks almost invariably go through the wall. To seal hairline cracks effectively, you must make flexible interior patches out of fiberglass cloth and asphalt sealer. You can seal cracks up to an inch wide with mastic joint sealer, which is heated with a propane torch until soft and pushed with a putty knife into the crack. The mastic is then covered with a patching mortar.

Of all the cracks in a basement, the most troublesome are those that occur where the floor meets the wall. Try filling them with a joint sealer and epoxy resin, which are in turn covered by mortar. If this remedy fails to keep the basement dry, the only solution is to install a sump pump *(pages 37-39)*.

Preventing seepage. Dampen the wall with a moist sponge and trowel on a ¼-inch layer of patching mortar mixed with a waterproofing additive such as silicone or latex. Work from the floor upward. After the cement dries but before it sets—about 20 minutes to one hour—use a stiff brush to apply a coat of waterproof cement paint, working the paint into the fresh cement.

PATCHING MORTAR

Patching stationary cracks. Open the crack with a cold chisel *(right)* until it is an inch wide, then remove loose concrete with a wire brush. Use a pointing trowel to wet the surfaces of the crack with patching mortar; then fill it with the mortar.

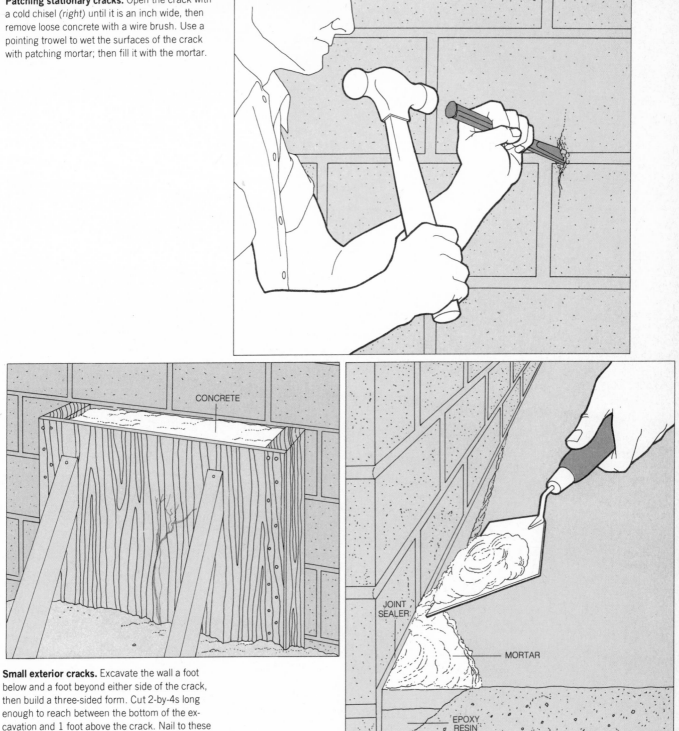

CONCRETE

JOINT SEALER

MORTAR

EPOXY RESIN

Small exterior cracks. Excavate the wall a foot below and a foot beyond either side of the crack, then build a three-sided form. Cut 2-by-4s long enough to reach between the bottom of the excavation and 1 foot above the crack. Nail to these edges ½-inch plywood the length of the 2-by-4s and 2 feet wider than the crack. Prop the form over the crack with 2-by-4 scraps and fill it with a standard concrete mix. Let the concrete set 24 hours before removing the form.

Filling wall-floor cracks. Widen the outside of the crack with a cold chisel, making a beveled slot. Dry the crack with a propane torch and line the slot next to the wall with a strip of mastic joint sealer ¼ inch thick to keep out moisture. Half fill the rest of the slot with epoxy resin to prevent the mastic from loosening, then mortar over the resin with a pointing trowel.

Repairing Small Moving Cracks

Repairing small moving cracks. Cut fiberglass cloth—the kind sold for patching walls—to cover the crack completely and extend at least 2 inches on all sides. Using detergent, clean the crack and the part of the wall to be covered by the patch. Brush on a coat of asphalt sealer, stick the patch to it, and cover it with more sealer.

Repairing Large Moving Cracks

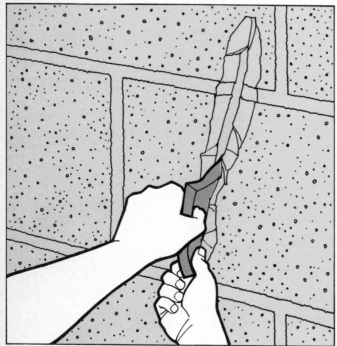

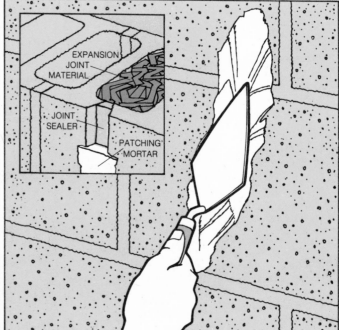

1 Preparing the crack. Chip out the crack so that it is ¾ inch wide at the bottom and 1 inch wide at the surface of the wall. If the wall is cinder block, cut strips of expansion joint material, an asphalt-impregnated substance used between sections of sidewalk. Stuff the material through the crack—using a screwdriver, if necessary—to fill the hollow inside the block.

2 Sealing the crack. Use a propane torch with a wide tip to heat mastic joint sealer until it is soft, then press it into the crack with a putty knife. Fill the crack about halfway, then, with a pointing trowel, fill the crack to the top with patching mortar to complete the job.

Plugging Flowing Leaks

1 **Inserting a bleeder hose.** Chip loose concrete away from the hole. Divert the water into a bucket by inserting a piece of rubber hose—any size that fits—and fill around it with dry hydraulic cement, which sets within a minute or two after it comes into contact with water. It is available in hardware stores.

2 **Inserting a plug.** When the hole around the hose is filled, shape a conical plug of dry hydraulic cement, hold it in the palm of one hand, pull out the bleeder hose and jam the plug into the hole, holding it in place until the cement sets.

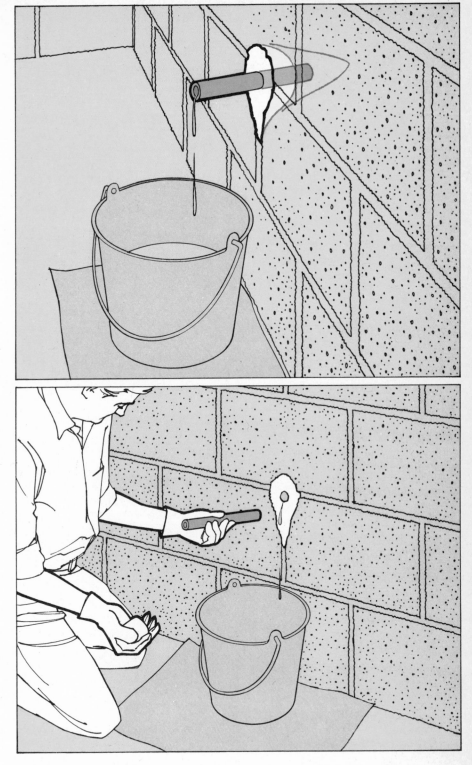

Exterior Waterproofing

If simple remedies, such as grading surface soil or patching interior walls, fail to cure a wet basement, you must block moisture outside the basement wall. No amount of interior patching will stop penetration caused by the power of substantial subsurface water pressure, nor will it plug leaks through cracks opened when the roots of a tree penetrate.

To waterproof a basement wall from the outside, you must excavate at least part of the foundation of the house, a heavy job you may want to have done. You also may prefer hiring a professional if basement walls must be resurfaced with concrete. But the rest of the job is fairly simple to do yourself.

Some cracks are shallow enough to block by simply excavating the upper part of the basement wall to a depth of about 2 feet and waterproofing with asphalt foundation coating and polyethylene plastic sheeting *(right)*. If the leak is lower down, there is no alternative to excavating the entire basement wall down to the footing. Once the digging is done, you should waterproof the wall with concrete and also lay drain tiles, which collect subsurface water and carry it away from the house. The tiles—made like storm-sewer piping, but generally perforated—are available in several materials in various lengths with connectors and elbow fittings. Tiles that are asphalt impregnated and rigid plastic types are the easiest to use.

Waterproofing near the surface. Dig a trench 4 feet wide and 2 feet deep around the house, sloping it downward away from the house. With a trowel, apply a coating of asphalt to the wall from the bottom of the ditch to grade level. Smooth the coating with a stiff brush. Then press a sheet of polyethylene plastic against the asphalt and extend the sheeting to line the bottom of the entire ditch. Fill the trench with a 1½-foot layer of rocks and cover with topsoil.

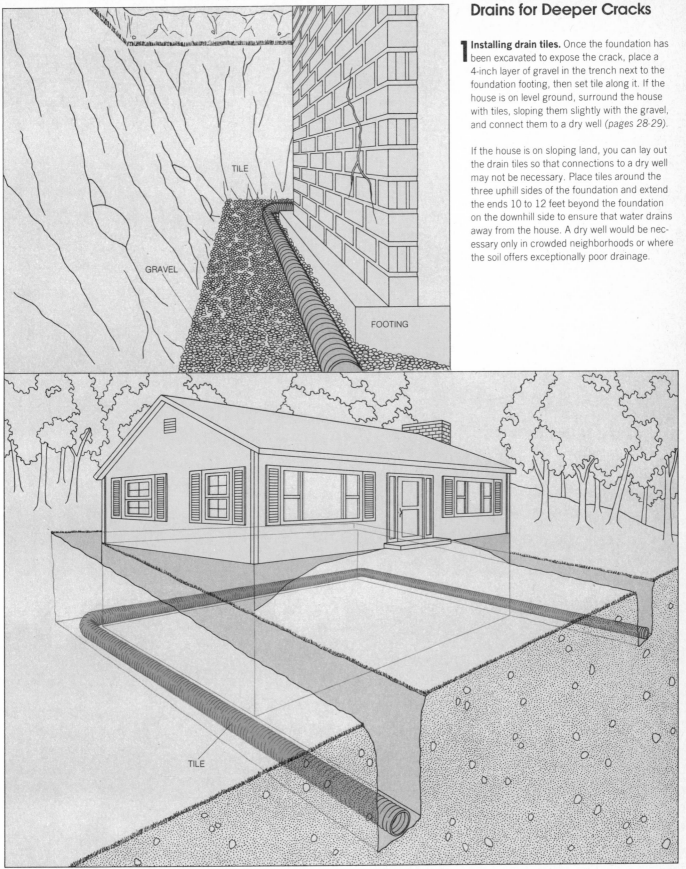

Drains for Deeper Cracks

1 Installing drain tiles. Once the foundation has been excavated to expose the crack, place a 4-inch layer of gravel in the trench next to the foundation footing, then set tile along it. If the house is on level ground, surround the house with tiles, sloping them slightly with the gravel, and connect them to a dry well (*pages 28-29*).

If the house is on sloping land, you can lay out the drain tiles so that connections to a dry well may not be necessary. Place tiles around the three uphill sides of the foundation and extend the ends 10 to 12 feet beyond the foundation on the downhill side to ensure that water drains away from the house. A dry well would be necessary only in crowded neighborhoods or where the soil offers exceptionally poor drainage.

TILE

GRAVEL

FOOTING

TILE

2 **Reinforcing the wall.** Begin by driving 6-inch lengths of ¼-inch metal reinforcing rods halfway into the old wall, putting one rod in each square foot of a 6-foot-square area around the crack. Put some rods into the crack and others in holes drilled with a masonry bit.

3 **Making the form.** Make a three-sided form to hold the concrete by nailing sheets of ½-inch plywood to a frame of 2-by-4s that is 6 feet wide and tall, and 4 inches deep. Set the form on the footing—open side to the wall as shown at far right—brace it firmly and pour the concrete. Remove the form after the concrete sets, reusing it as needed on other exterior cracks.

4 **Adding asphalt.** With a trowel, apply a layer of asphalt to the new concrete and smooth it with a stiff brush. Press polyethylene plastic sheeting on the asphalt. The sheeting can extend above-ground and be trimmed after the ditch is filled.

5 **Finishing and filling.** Bury the tile in gravel in a pile inclined against the footing as shown at far right. Fill the ditch and replace the sod.

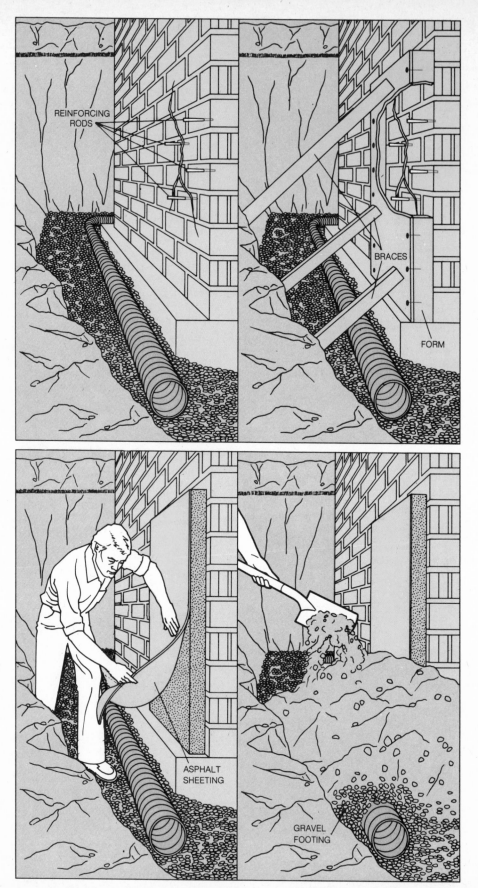

If All Else Fails, a Sump Pump

In some cases, the best solution to a wet-basement problem is not sealing the foundation but installing a sump pump that will expel water as fast as it enters. A sump pump may be preferable to expensive foundation repairs if, for example, basement flooding only occurs during severe storms. And it is the only practical remedy if water is being forced up through the basement floor by a rising water table. In addition to solving immediate problems, a pump is good insurance against water damage from burst pipes or backed-up basement drains.

Sump pumps come in many versions. Most are permanently installed units that run on electricity, but they may also be powered by small gasoline engines or by pressure from the water main, and they are sometimes intended for occasional emergency duty rather than regular use. Sump pumps empty water that runs into a hole, or sump, dug in the lowest part of the basement. The pump starts automatically as the water level in the sump rises, then switches itself off when the water has been evacuated.

Installing a sump pump is an interdisciplinary task, typically calling for the skills of a plumber, electrician and carpenter, as illustrated overleaf. The first part of the job is to dig the sump. To chop through the concrete floor of most basements, you can rent an electric jackhammer from a tool rental agency. The sump will have to accommodate a liner —a bottomless cylinder, available from plumbing suppliers in a variety of materials, that prevents the sides of the hole from caving in. A liner should have a diameter of at least 15 inches; a smaller liner with less water capacity will shorten the life of a pump by causing it to operate more frequently. Before purchasing the liner check the pump manufacturer's instructions for any recommendations on sump diameter and depth.

In making plans for a discharge line, first consult your local plumbing code. Most communities will not allow you to pump basement water into sewer lines, but many will not object if you pipe the water to the storm drain system. Or you can simply pump the water away from the house and let it disperse through the soil. Sump pumps usually require 1¼- or 1½-inch discharge piping. Use a plastic pipe if possible; it is easier to work with.

Manufacturers of electric sump pumps usually recommend that power be drawn from a separate, unswitched outlet. Such a source can safely supply the large amounts of current required to start most pumps, and it will also ensure that the pump cannot be unintentionally disconnected by flipping off a basement light switch. Before installing a new receptacle, check your local electrical code to be sure that you use the correct materials. Call in an electrician to make the connection at the service panel.

Every sump should have a cover in order to keep out pump-clogging debris and eliminate the possibility of injuries caused by unexpectedly stepping into an open hole. Some sump liners can be purchased with a cover, but in most cases you must make your own (page 39).

Two common pumps. Electric sump pumps are available in two basic forms—pedestal (below, left) and submersible (right). Both have a rotary pump unit that rests on the floor of the sump. Water enters through a grill, which traps objects that could damage the pump, and leaves from an outlet to which a discharge pipe is attached. The submersible pump, completely sealed against water and installed below the floor of the basement, is quieter than a pedestal model, which has a less expensive, unsealed motor atop a long stalk to keep from getting wet. A float near the base of the stalk is connected to a switch that turns on the motor when the water rises above a predetermined level; a submersible pump is controlled by a switch inside the motor.

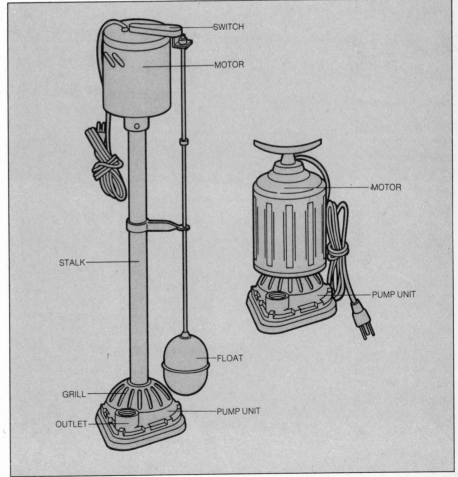

Preparing the Sump

1 Digging the sump. With chalk and a piece of string, mark a circle on the basement floor where water collects. The circle should measure 3 inches larger in diameter than the sump liner you are using and, if possible, should lie close to a wall and out of the way. With an electric jackhammer from a tool-rental agency, chop through the basement floor around the sump outline, then deepen the sump with a shovel until the hole is about 2 inches deeper than the liner.

If water collects in more than one depression in the floor, use a chalk line to lay out drainage trenches, about 2 inches wide, to the sump; use the jackhammer to dig them 1 to 2 inches deep.

3 Installing a discharge pipe. For the outlet through the foundation, choose a side of the house where soil provides good drainage. Inside the basement, about 10 inches below ground level, make a hole through the wall large enough for the discharge pipe. Use the rented jackhammer if the foundation is concrete, or a 4-pound maul and cold chisel if it is cinder block.

Outside, locate the outlet hole by digging at the foundation. Push a 2-foot length of discharge pipe through the hole in the wall so it protrudes equally on either side. On the outer end of this pipe, install a check valve—with the arrow pointed away from the basement—to prevent backup of water and to intercept any small animals. Excavate a trench 1 or 2 feet wide to hold perforated drain tubing or, if the soil offers poor drainage, to lead unperforated tubing to a dry well or storm sewer (*pages 28-29*). The trench floor should be inclined away from the house so water will not collect and freeze in the tubing in winter.

Inside the basement, extend the discharge pipe horizontally toward the sump. For a short run to a nearby sump, the discharge pipe can jut directly from the wall, as shown at right. Discharge pipes more than 3 or 4 feet long should be strapped to the wall or the overhead joists for support, according to the manufacturer's recommendation. About 3 inches from the center of the sump, use an elbow to turn the pipe toward the pump.

Pack mortar around the discharge pipe where it passes through the foundation, sealing the wall.

2 Lining the hole. To keep the pump from sinking into the mud and becoming clogged, lay a 4-inch bed of gravel at the bottom of the sump. Next, slide the liner into the sump and pack dirt between the liner and the side of the hole. Fill the last few inches with mortar and trowel smooth, being careful not to dam any drainage trenches leading to the sump. Mix enough mortar to smooth the inner surfaces of the trenches.

GROUND LEVEL

COUPLING

ELBOW

CHECK VALVE

DISCHARGE PIPE

MORTAR

4 **Supplying electricity for the pump.** String three-wire plastic-sheathed cable from the service panel, along the joists, to a point above the sump. Strap the cable to walls and joists every 4 feet and whenever it turns corners. On the joist above the pump, fasten a surface-mounted electrical box that has a cable connector fitted through a knockout. Thread the cable through the connector; trim the cable so 8 inches stick out.

Strip the sheathing from the tail, and remove ¾ inch of insulation from the black and white wires in the cable. Attach the black wire to the brass terminal of a grounded receptacle and the white wire to the silver terminal. With a wire cap, attach two 4-inch green or bare jumper wires to the bare wire in the cable; then, with a sheet-metal screw, connect one of the jumpers to the green terminal of the receptacle and the other to the box. Attach the receptacle to the box and close it with a cover plate. Have an electrician connect the other end of the cable to the service panel through a ground-fault interrupter, a circuit breaker that prevents serious shocks.

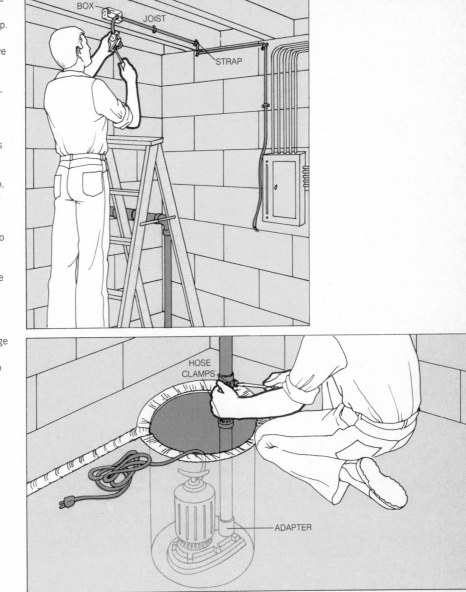

5 **Installing the pump.** Screw a length of discharge pipe, fitted with a threaded adapter, into the pump outlet. The pipe should be long enough to extend a few inches above the lip of the sump when the pump is in position. Lower the pump into the sump and connect the pieces of discharge pipe to each other with rubber hose and hose clamps if the pipes are plastic; use a coupling called a union if the pipes are metal.

6 **Making a cover.** From a piece of ¾-inch plywood, cut a square with sides extending about 6 inches beyond the edges of the sump. Draw a line across the middle of the square. Along this line, cut a slot wide enough to fit the discharge pipe and deep enough so that the cover overlaps the edge of the sump evenly all around. If the cause of basement flooding is seepage through the walls, screw strips of the plywood along two opposite edges of the cover to raise it off the basement floor and allow water to reach the sump. Before installing the cover, paint it and tape the pump's electrical cord to the discharge pipe.

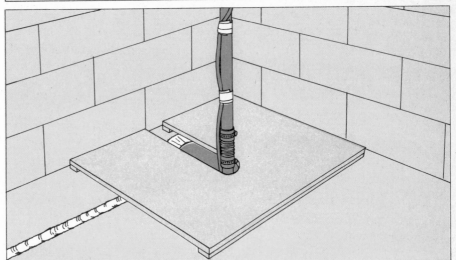

39

Roof Leaks: Hard to Find, Easy to Fix

The old joke that a roof leaks only during a rain, when you can't fix it, is at least half wrong—the trickiest part of repairing a leak is finding it, and that may be easier when the water is coming through. Even then, do not assume the damage is near the drip, for the multiple-layer construction of modern roofs (below) can lead water on a long and twisting course over several layers and through joints before it finally pours out into the house. Often it will travel down inside a second-story wall, across a first-floor ceiling and gush out around a lighting fixture.

Some leaks are caused by tears or punctures in the roofing surface, which you may be able to see from outside. Curled shingles, which admit wind-blown rain, are another visible cause. In winter, ice build-up on eaves can result in leaks (page 50). But equally common—and generally undetectable by inspection—are small openings in the metal flashing that should be installed at vents, chimneys, and corners or angles. The inevi-table expansion and contraction of house parts loosens the sealant—called roofing cement—that covers the edges of flashing. The cement may also crumble with age, and it should be checked and renewed every few years.

Although a leak may be far from the drip, start your exploration there. Look for damage to the roof in the general area overhead. Or try to trace the leak from interior signs—even slight discoloration in a wall or ceiling suggests moisture. In an unfinished attic, you may be able to see gaps in the roofing from inside; look for pinpoints of daylight, and if you find a spot, mark it by poking a wire through. Remember that leaks may also arise in house siding, generally at cracks, breaks or vertical butt joints.

On the roof itself, always take on jobs of preventive maintenance as well as patching existing leaks. Check the flashings and reseal them if necessary (pages 48-49)—the same technique will work for leaks in a roof made entirely of metal —and replace missing or damaged shingles. The shingles that you are most likely to work with will be asphalt—low cost and light weight have made asphalt shingles (opposite) the most commonly used roofing material in the United States and Canada. Consisting of a felt base that is saturated with asphalt and coated with mineral granules, these shingles normally last anywhere from 15 to 25 years. And because they are relatively flexible, asphalt shingles are simpler for the amateur to repair or replace than are slate or wood shingles, which call for certain specialized techniques (pages 43-45).

Asphalt shingles are packaged in bundles containing about 27 strips, 3 feet wide, and each composed of two or three shingle tabs separated by cutouts. Three bundles make a "square"—enough shingles to cover 100 square feet of roof surface. Although most shingles are sold by the square, many home-repair centers or lumberyards will sell bundles or even individual shingles.

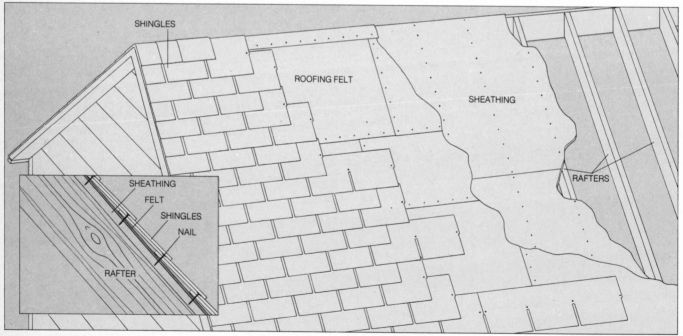

The anatomy of a roof. To provide a firm base for roofing materials, rafters are covered with sheathing—usually 1-by-6-inch boards or, on newer homes, 4-by-8-foot sheets of plywood. Overlapping layers of roofing felt or building paper are nailed or stapled to the sheathing, and the overlapping rows, or courses, of shingles are fastened with roofing nails that penetrate the underlying shingles as well as the felt and the sheathing (inset). The tortuous path of water through these layers can make the source of a leak hard to find. When water leaks beneath a damaged shingle, it may soak directly through the underlying felt or flow downward until it reaches a loose seam or damaged area. At the sheathing, the water will generally run down to the joint between adjoining boards or plywood sheets, then along the joint to a loose butt joint over a rafter. Finally, the water may run along the rafter for a distance before dripping to the floor —far from the original hole in the shingle.

Repairing Asphalt Shingles

Reseating wind-blown shingles. If high winds lift or curl the tabs of asphalt shingles, wind-driven rain can penetrate the opened space beneath. To secure lifted tabs, use a caulking gun *(page 18)* to apply dabs of quick-setting shingle cement under the tab, then press it down into the cement. When replacing shingles, use the wind-resistant type, which has factory-applied adhesive on the upper surface an inch above the cutouts. After installation, the adhesive is softened by the heat of the sun, and holds the overlapping shingles in place.

Sealing small tears. If the damage does not extend under the overlapping shingles, coat the underside with roofing cement and press it flat. Nail both sides of the tear with 1-inch roofing nails and cover both the nailheads and the tear with additional cement. To replace a badly torn shingle, see the instructions on page 42.

Some Dos and Don'ts for Roofing Work

Working on a pitched roof is potentially dangerous: if you fear heights or if your roof is steeply pitched, the job is best left to a professional. But you can make repairs safely by taking these common-sense precautions:

☐ Never work in wet, windy or cold weather. Roofing materials can become dangerously slippery when wet, and asphalt shingles are brittle when cold, crumbling underfoot.

☐ Wear sneakers or shoes that have slip-resistant soles, and choose loose-fitting clothes so that you can move about freely.

☐ Use an access ladder that extends above the eave so that you need never step over the top of the ladder. Keep your hips between the rails as you climb, and never lean over the side of the ladder to work on the roof.

☐ Enlist a helper to steady the ladder as you climb and to feed you tools and materials once you are up there.

☐ On a steep roof, use a roofing ladder with wood or metal brackets that hook over the roof ridge *(below)*. These ladders not only provide secure hand- and footholds, but distribute your weight over the shingles. On brittle roofing materials such as slate, tile or asbestos, use a "chicken ladder" of the kind shown on page 43 —a 1-by-12-inch board with 1-by-2-inch horizontal wood cleats.

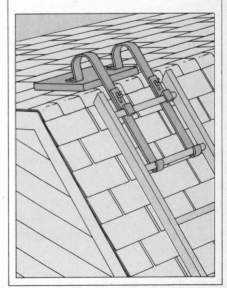

Replacing Asphalt Shingles

1 Removing the nails. To free a damaged shingle, you must pry out two rows of nails: a lower row on the damaged shingle, and an upper row that fastens both the shingle above and the upper edge of the damaged shingle. Each row usually consists of four nails, none of which are ordinarily visible. To get at the upper row, raise the shingle tabs two courses above the damaged shingle; insert the flat end of a pry bar under the nails thus exposed and remove them. Lifting the course above the damaged shingle will expose the second row of nails for removal with the pry bar.

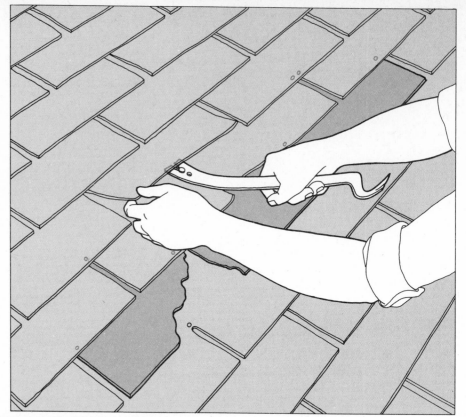

2 Removing the damaged shingle. Carefully pull out the damaged shingle. If it resists, make sure you have loosened all the nails holding it in place; then, with a putty knife, gently pry it away from the shingles above and below it. With the old shingle removed, apply roofing cement to all tears or holes in the shingle or roofing felt underneath.

3 Installing the new shingle. Slide the shingle into place, aligning its bottom edge with the adjacent ones in its course. Then lift the second course above to expose the old nail holes in the first course above. Use these nail holes, nailing from one end of the shingle to the other to avoid buckling. To avoid curling the lifted tabs, do not try to lift the tabs high enough for hammering directly; instead, slide the flat end of a pry bar over the nailhead and hammer the bar just clear of the shingle's bottom edge *(above)*. For the lower nails, use the pry bar again to lift the first course above and to drive the nails. Locate two of them ⅝ inch above the cutouts separating the tabs, and the other two an inch in from the edges.

Slate and Wood Shingle Roofs

Slate and wood shingles are not only two of the most attractive roofing materials, but when properly installed and maintained, they are exceptionally durable. And when repair is necessary, one or two pieces, rather than a whole strip, can be replaced. Follow the safety precautions on page 41 when working on either type of roof, and be especially careful on a slate roof: slate is brittle and it is extremely slippery when wet.

Lay wood shingles and shakes—thick hand-split shingles—with a ¼-inch spacing on either side to allow for expansion as they swell with moisture. You may find that the shingles were originally installed on spaced sheathing boards rather than solid sheathing; the open space beneath the shingles provides ventilation to dry out the wood. When cracks and splits do appear, act quickly. Work from a chicken ladder securely anchored at the ridge with roof hooks like those on page 41. Seal a small split or make a temporary re-

pair on wood or slate *(below)*. If a shingle is badly split or rotted, replace it with a matching one. The job will go faster if you use a roofing tool called a slate puller; if you cannot get one, use a hacksaw blade to cut the nails *(page 44)*.

Moss, which speeds decay, is a common problem on wood roofs, particularly in shady areas or damp climates. Scrape the moss off with a stiff brush and paint the affected area with a commercial wood preservative.

Loose slates are usually caused either by rusted nails or by cracks and breaks in the slate itself. Rusted nails can mean you need professional reroofing: the installer did not use corrosion-resistant nails, as he should have. Cracks or breaks are most likely to occur in relatively porous, moisture-absorbing slates; during winter freezes, the water expands and cracks the slate. You can fill hairline cracks with roofing compound, but badly cracked or broken slates must be replaced.

Quick fix with a metal patch. To keep a split wood shingle from leaking—or to repair a badly damaged shingle or slate temporarily—make a patch from a sheet of copper or aluminum flashing. With a pair of metal shears, cut the patch to twice the width and about 3 inches longer than the exposed length of the damaged shingle. Apply roofing cement to the center of the patch, and slide the patch up and under the damaged shingle, cemented side down. Continue pushing the patch upward, using a wood block and hammer to tap it if necessary, until its top edge passes the butt of the shingles in the next course.

CHICKEN LADDER

BUTT

WOOD BLOCK

METAL PATCH

Replacing Wood Shingles

1 **Removing the shingle.** Using a mallet and a wood chisel, split the damaged shingle along the end grain to break it into narrow strips and slivers. Then lift the end of each strip, work it from side to side to break it away from the hidden nails and pull it free.

2 **Cutting the nails.** The two nails that hold the damaged shingle in place are normally hidden, located about an inch from the edges of the shingle and about 2 inches up underneath the butt of the overlapping shingle. To remove them, use a slate puller (*opposite, top left*), if you have one. Or slip a long hacksaw blade under the overlapping shingle and cut through the nails flush with the shingle or sheathing beneath it. Protect your hand with a glove or by wrapping the blade end in heavy masking tape.

3 **Installing the new shingle.** To allow for expansion, use a replacement shingle ½ inch narrower than the space it will fill—trim the new shingle if necessary, using a hand plane or a small hatchet. Tap the shingle into place with a wood block and hammer; if any nails in the upper courses obstruct the new shingle, shorten it by cutting across its tapered end. Align the butt of the new shingle with the others in its course, then secure it with two galvanized roofing nails ¾ inch from each edge and just below the overlapping shingle. Coat the nailheads with roofing cement.

Replacing Broken Slates

1 **Removing the damaged slate.** Slide the end of a slate puller under the damaged slate and hook one of the two sharp puller notches around a nail holding the slate in place. With a hammer, strike sharply down against the puller handle to cut through the nail; repeat on the other nail and pull the damaged slate free. If you have no slate puller, use a hacksaw blade (*left, center*).

2 **Cutting a new slate to size.** Using the damaged slate as a guide, mark both sides of the replacement. Score along the lines on each side repeatedly with a cold chisel. Set a scored line at the edge of a flat surface and snap off the excess. Smooth the edges with emery cloth.

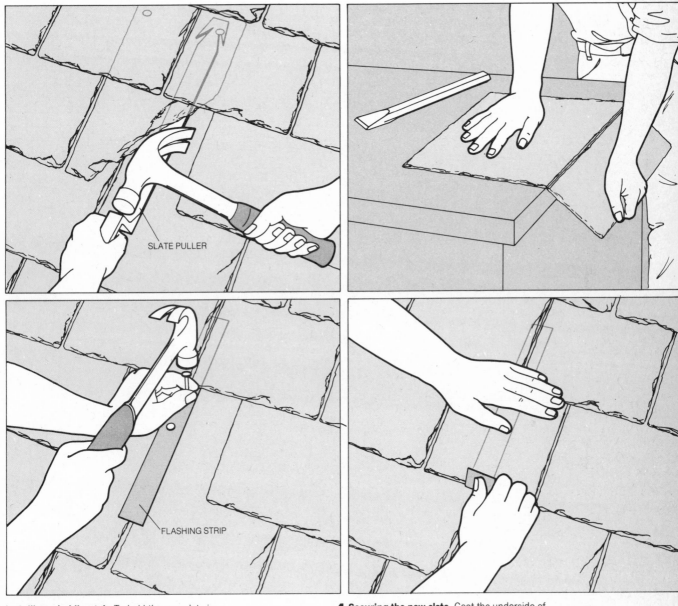

SLATE PULLER

FLASHING STRIP

3 **Installing a holding tab.** To hold the new slate in place, cut a strip of copper or aluminum flashing 2 inches wide and long enough to run for several inches under the slates above the damaged one and about 2 inches below the bottom edge of the replacement slate. Fasten the strip onto the joint between the underlying slates, using nails of the same metal as the flashing.

4 **Securing the new slate.** Coat the underside of the replacement slate with roofing cement and slide it into position over the holding tab and under the slates in the course above. Bend the holding tab up around the bottom edge of the slate, and secure it with a dab of cement.

Repairing Flat Roofs

Roofs that are flat or nearly flat usually are built up with as many as five alternating layers of roofing felt and hot tar or asphalt, fastened to the wood sheathing. This built-up roofing is often topped with a protective covering of gravel, pebbles or marble chips, or with a final layer of mineral-surfaced roll roofing; the light-colored stones or minerals help reflect the sun's rays from the dark, heat-absorbent surface.

A built-up roof should last from 10 to 20 years, before the sun's heat dries out the tar or asphalt and cracks develop over the entire surface. You can extend its life considerably by coating it with an asphalt-aluminum roof paint that slows the drying process and forms a stronger and more reflective surface.

When the roof does eventually fail, do not try to replace it yourself—that job calls for special equipment and the expertise of a professional roofer. But you can and should repair minor damages. Inspect the roof at least once a year for blisters, cracks, tears and storm damage. Blisters, which indicate that roofing felt has separated from the underlying layers or from the wood sheathing, should be treated immediately by the method shown at right, before they break open and admit rain water.

As you treat a blister, examine its interior. If it is dry, the blister is probably caused by poorly adhering or dried-out asphalt cement, and a simple patch can be an adequate repair. Interior moisture is a sign that water has leaked into the roofing and seeped along the sheathing to a point underneath the blister. Locate the point of leakage—possibly in loose flashings *(page 48)* at adjoining walls or around chimneys and vent pipes. If a substantial amount of water has penetrated the roofing, causing a large section to buckle or blister, cut out and patch the entire area *(opposite)*.

Treating a Blister

1 **Cutting the blister open.** Use a stiff brush to sweep dirt and loose gravel or mineral granules away from the blistered area. Then slice the blister open lengthwise with a hook-nosed linoleum knife *(right)* or a utility knife. If the felt layers beneath the surface are dry, proceed directly to Step 2. If they are damp, deepen the cut down to the wood sheathing and let the roofing dry out (you can use a portable electric heater-fan or hair drier to speed the process) before proceeding to Step 2. To locate the source of the leak, feel for the spongy lines or patches leading from the blister to a faulty flashing or other damaged area. In that area make the more extensive repair that is shown opposite.

2 **Sealing the cut.** Use a putty knife to work asphalt roofing cement under both sides of the cut. Press the layers of roofing material flat against the sheathing and nail each side with 1½-inch flathead roofing nails, ¾ inch apart.

3 **Patching the cut.** Cut a patch of 15-pound roofing felt large enough to overlap the blistered area about 2 inches in every direction. Cover an equivalent area over the cut with roofing cement and press the patch into place. Fasten the patch at its edges with 1½-inch roofing nails, and cover the nailheads and the edges of the patch with additional roofing cement.

Putting In a Patch

1 Removing the damaged section. Begin the repair of a large tear or a large blistered or buckled area by scraping off any gravel coating around the damaged area; then cut out a square or rectangle that includes the damage. Dip your knife in turpentine as you work to keep the blade free of tar and felt fibers, and pull out the layers of felt individually. If water has soaked the felt, remove all the roofing within the rectangle, down to the sheathing, and dry the area thoroughly as shown in Step 1, opposite.

2 Rebuilding the roofing. Using one of the damaged layers as a guide, cut matching patches from new 15-pound roofing felt—one patch for each layer you have removed. Coat the bottom of the exposed roofing with asphalt cement, and work additional cement under the edges of the adjoining material. Lay a felt patch in the cement bed, press it into place, and coat its top with a bed of cement. Continue rebuilding the roofing layer by layer until it is level with the surrounding area. Nail the top patch down with 1½-inch roofing nails spaced evenly around the edges.

3 Adding a protective covering. If the original roofing was covered with a layer of mineral-surfaced roll roofing, cut an oversized patch of the same material and press it into a bed of asphalt cement over the patched area. Nail down the edges of the patch and cover the nailheads and patch edges with cement. If the finish consists of gravel or marble chips, spread a thick layer of roofing cement over the top patch of roofing felt, sprinkle gravel or chips over the cement, and press the stones firmly into the cement with a flat board.

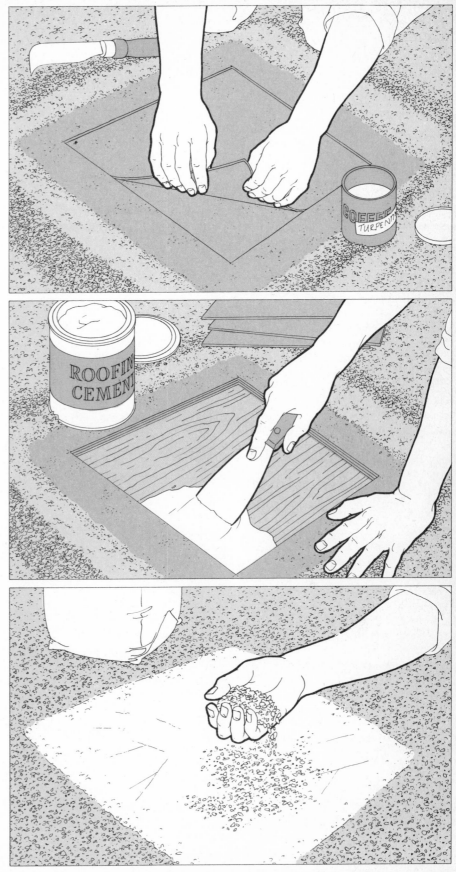

Flashing for the Weak Points

The weakest points in a roof, from a weatherproofing viewpoint, are the angles where slopes meet to form a valley and where chimneys and vent pipes project through the roofing. To protect these vulnerable areas, flashing is installed to make watertight seals between adjoining structures or surfaces. But without regular inspection and preventive maintenance, any flashing can become a funnel directing water into your home instead of the gutters and downspouts.

The best flashings are of rust-resistant metals such as copper, aluminum or zinc. Some older homes have galvanized-steel flashings. The life of more rust-prone flashings can be lengthened considerably if rust spots are removed promptly with a wire brush and the flashings are painted periodically with metal primer and aluminum paint. Metal flashings also are damaged by galvanic corrosion caused by an electrochemical reaction at spots where dissimilar metals meet; when repairing or replacing flashings, make sure the new metal and nails are the same materials as the old.

As a less-expensive substitute for metal, some roofers use a double layer of mineral-surfaced roll roofing in valleys. Roof valleys take some of the hardest wear because they channel water from two roof slopes to the gutters. When inspecting valley flashings for leaks, remember that water can flow or seep uphill because of wind patterns or a heavier flow off one slope backing up the other side. The roofing cement sealing the shingle to the flashing needs to be inspected and renewed regularly.

Chimney flashing, most often copper, is more complex and more vulnerable to leaks than other roof flashings. In the best installations a set of base flashings is secured to the roof sheathing and a set of overlapping cap flashings is embedded in the brickwork of the chimney. This construction allows slight movement and settlement without damage to the waterproofing seal. However, many chimney flashings consist of single metal pieces whose upper edge is set into the brick joints or simply cemented to the side of the chimney. The methods of repair are similar for both types.

The commonest problem with chimney flashings is deterioration of mortar or other seals; water then runs behind the top edge of the flashing and down the chimney into the house. Loose mortar should be replaced and all flashing joints resealed with asphalt cement (opposite, top). Flashing that is loose or worn around a vent pipe is equally serious, but new presized metal and plastic pipe flashings make replacement more practical than repairs. These flashings fit common pipes and include rubber collars to form a watertight joint without caulking (opposite, bottom).

FLASHING EDGE

METAL FLASHING

ROOFING CEMENT

Repairing valley flashing. If watermarks or other signs of damage are found inside the attic under the valley, inspect the flashing for holes. Repair holes in metal flashing by cleaning around the hole with a wire brush, coating the area with a thin layer of roofing cement and pressing a matching metal patch into the cement. The patch should overlap the hole several inches all around; seal the edges of the patch with additional cement. Fix tears in roll roofing flashing with asphalt cement and felt patches, following the instructions for repairing built-up roofs (pages 46-47).

If there is no visible damage to the flashing itself, the asphalt cement sealing it to the shingles probably has worked loose, allowing water to seep under. Starting at the eaves, pack roofing cement under the shingle edges with a putty knife (above) and press the shingles flat; do not nail shingles within 6 inches of the valley center.

Resealing a Chimney

1 Cleaning the mortar joint. Pry the loose cap flashings out of the mortar joint and lay them aside. Using a cold chisel and mallet, remove an inch and a half of mortar from the joint. Check that the top edge of the exposed base flashing is flush with the brickwork and seal the edge with roofing cement as necessary.

2 Installing the flashing. Dampen the open joint with a wet brush and insert the lip of the cap flashing in the joint. Using a tool called a joint filler *(below)*, slide mortar off the edge of a board and tamp it into the joint, filling the space. When the mortar is firm but not hard, finish by shaping it to match the other joints.

3 Sealing the joints. Inspect the rest of the chimney for any crumbling mortar joints and repair them following Steps 1 and 2. Then seal all of the joints and overlaps with a liberal coating of roofing cement, extending the cement 2 inches out on either side of the joints.

Resealing a Vent Pipe

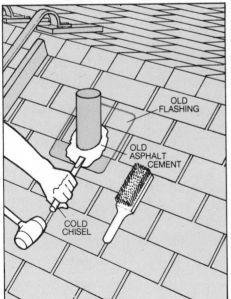
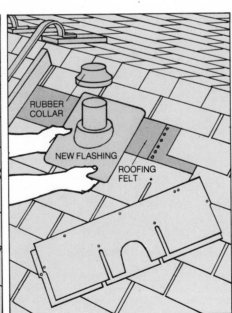

1 Removing the old flashing. Chip away the seal around the pipe. Expose the sides and upper portion of the flashing by removing the two shingle strips immediately above the pipe. Loosen the higher shingle first *(Step 1, page 42)*. Remove any nails and loosen any cement holding the old flashing to the roof; if it is stuck to the roofing felt, cut away the felt and replace it by nailing a patch of 15-pound felt to the roof. Lift the flashing over the pipe and discard it.

2 Installing the new flashing. Seal all existing nail holes with roofing cement. Clean cement residue from the vent pipe with a wire brush and slide the new metal flashing down over the pipe until the flange is flush with the roofing. Then push the rubber collar down the pipe until it is flush with the metal flashing.

3 Replacing the shingles. Reinstall the shingle strips removed in Step 1, beginning with the lower shingle that overlaps the sides and back of the flashing. Follow the instructions for installing new shingles on page 42, but do not drive nails through the metal flange. Instead, seal the shingle edges to the metal with roofing cement.

Thwarting Snow and Ice

Icicles hanging from the eaves of a house are a lovely sight after a fresh snowfall, but they can be hazardous both to passersby and to your house. Large icicles can weigh 50 pounds or more—enough, if they fall, to cause injury to someone standing below. Moreover, they can pull gutters out of alignment or dislodge them from the eaves.

Icicles may also be a sign of an ice dam, a wall of ice along the edge of the roof caused when melted water from snow above refreezes on the eave. Once the dam forms, water accumulates behind it, working its way under shingles and into the house. The best solution for ice dams is to prevent them; if the roof is properly insulated and the attic adequately ventilated *(pages 78-85 and pages 52-58),* the roof will not get warm enough to melt snow that may refreeze lower down. There are, however, additional remedies. One is a wide strip of flashing, nailed in place of the shingles at the edge of a roof where there are no gutters *(right, top).* Ice and snow slide from the roof before they become a problem. For an eave with a gutter, a better solution is to string outdoor heating cable, which is available in kits designed especially for the purpose, along the eave to keep the roof edge free of ice *(opposite).*

In areas of heavy snowfall you may want to reinforce the rafters to prevent your roof from sagging—or even collapsing—after a blizzard. A 4-foot snowfall on a 20-by-30-foot roof weighs 30 tons, as much as a DC-9 airplane. Although such strengthening is unnecessary in homes built to the specifications of modern building codes, it may be advisable if you suspect your house was skimped on. If your house has 2-inch-by-6-inch rafters longer than 13 feet or 2-inch-by-8-inch rafters longer than 17½ feet, you may want to install the knee studs shown at bottom right, just to be on the safe side.

Flashing the eave. Before starting, read the safety tips for working on a roof *(page 41).* Then remove the bottom two rows of shingles along the eave, using the technique shown on page 42 for asphalt shingles, page 44 for wood shingles and page 45 for slate. Slide a strip of flashing under the third row of shingles until it hits the nails holding them to the roof. The flashing must be wide enough to extend at least ½ inch beyond the fascia board. Use galvanized roofing nails every 6 inches to fasten the flashing to the roof sheathing just below the third course of shingles and along the eave. If you must use more than one piece of flashing, overlap them 6 inches and secure each seam with two rows of nails. Cover each nailhead and seam with roofing cement.

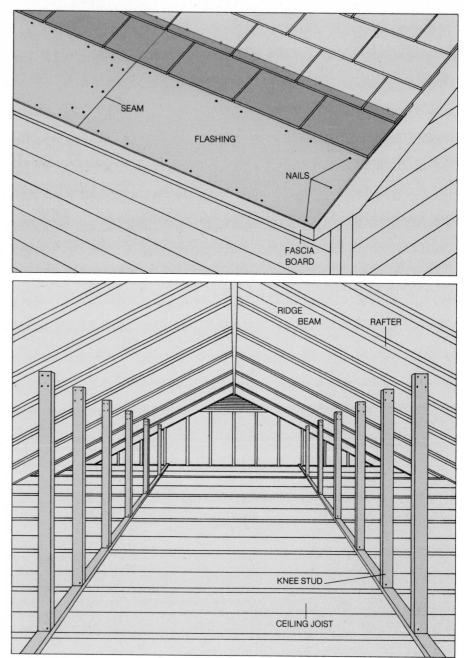

Installing knee studs. Measure the length of a rafter from the exterior wall to the ridge beam. For a storage attic, drop a plumb line from the midpoint of each rafter, and mark the tops of the joists or the flooring where the line touches. Use 16-penny nails to attach a 2-by-4 floor plate at that distance from the wall on each side of the attic. For each rafter cut a 2-by-4 knee stud long enough to extend from the floor plate and overlap the side of the rafter. Toenail each stud to the plate, then secure it to the rafter side above. If you plan a live-in attic, set the knee studs one third the rafter-length from the exterior walls and install collar beams *(page 80, Step 1).*

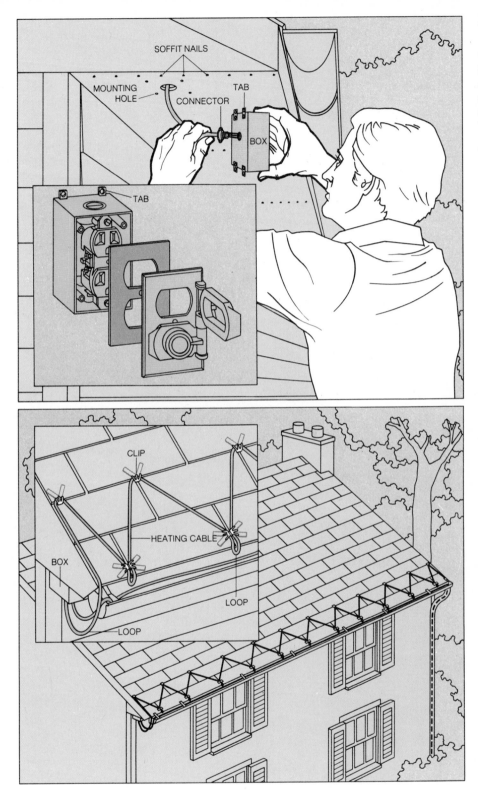

A Heater to De-ice Gutters

Wiring a circuit. To install outdoor cable, you will have to run a wire from a house circuit to an outdoor box mounted on the soffit. First, use the box as a template to mark the soffit for a cable hole and for mounting-screw holes. Hold the box between two rows of soffit nails and mark holes for mounting screws and a 1⅛-inch hole for the cable. Drill the holes.

After turning off the power, extend an indoor circuit through a switch and out the cable hole. Attach a two-part connector to the cable and screw the box to the connector. Mount the box on the soffit; because of the connector's shape, you may have to enlarge the cable hole with a rasp to align the tabs with the screw holes.

Connect a receptacle—preferably one with a shock-protection device called a ground-fault interrupter (GFI)—to the cable. Fasten the black wire to the brass terminal (or black wire of a GFI), white wire to the silver terminal (white wire of a GFI) and bare wire to the green terminal (green wire of a GFI). Mount the receptacle in the box and seal it with an outdoor cover plate (*inset*).

Mounting the cables. Most eaves require two heating-cable kits, one for the gutter and downspout, and one for the roof. One cable should equal the combined lengths of the gutter and the downspout. To calculate the roof-cable length, multiply the length of the gutter either by 1.8, 2.6 or 3.5, depending on whether the cable is to cover a 1-, 2- or 3-foot overhang.

Place the cable clips supplied with the kit underneath the shingles (*inset*) if they are asphalt; if shingles are wood or slate, glue on the clips with epoxy cement. Position the roof cable so it loops down from the shingles into the gutter. Lay the other cable in the gutter and drop one end into the downspout. Do not shorten the cables or allow them to touch or cross each other. Plug in the cables, leaving a loop of wire so rain and melted snow will drip away from the receptacle.

The Indispensable Openings: Vents for Air Flow

To an uninstructed eye, the only openings in a house are the windows and doors. In reality a substantial number of vented openings are deliberately cut into the roof, walls and basement of a well-constructed house to allow hot or moist air to escape and to draw cooler or drier air in from the outside.

In the basement, vents in the foundation walls keep condensation from forming on beams in the basement and inside the ground-floor walls *(page 59)*. You can install small vents in the siding to keep moisture from accumulating behind the wall sheathing and damaging wood and paint, although construction experts now recommend instead that interior walls be painted with glossy oil-base enamel to create a vapor barrier, followed by a coat of alkyd paint.

Attic venting is most important of all.

An unventilated attic is a year-round problem, even if it is insulated from the rest of the house. On hot summer days, attic temperatures can reach 135° to 150°, keeping the rest of the house hot long after sundown and putting a heavy—and expensive—load on air conditioners. In winter, when the house is heated but the attic is cold, condensation can form inside upper walls and ceilings adjacent to the attic, which can rot wood, insulation, paint and plaster.

A steady flow of air through the attic, provided by a combination of the vents shown below, solves both problems by removing hot air in the summer and water vapor in the winter. Most of these vents are easily installed by cutting through the sheathing of a house in or near the roof. However, ridge and cupola vents *(page 58)* call for the skill of a professional because of the amount of cutting that must be done.

If practical to install, vents in the soffit —the underside of the roof edge—are effective because they permit fresh air to enter the attic at a low level and rise, carrying heat or moisture up to be expelled through vents in the gables *(pages 54-55)*, the roof ridge *(page 58)* or in the roof itself *(pages 56-57)*. While not all houses are suited to soffit venting, all require venting near the roof peak. For adequate air flow if there are no vapor barriers *(page 71)* between the attic and the rest of the house, install 1 square foot of vent area for every 150 square feet of attic floor. If there are vapor barriers, install 1 square foot of vent area for every 300 square feet of attic floor. Half the vent area should be in the soffits, if possible, and the rest in the roof or gables.

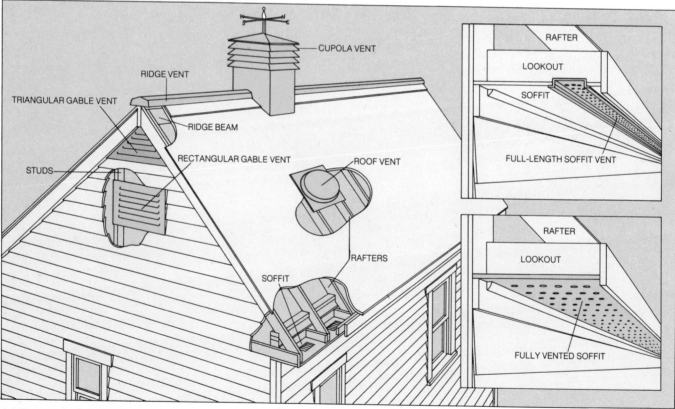

A full range of roof vents. No single house would be fitted with all the openings in this drawing, which is meant as a general guide to the vents described here and on the following pages.
Soffit vents fit into the wooden panel, or soffit, that covers the underside of an eave. The single type is easier to install, but the full-length strip type is more effective; most effective of all is the fully vented soffit, with openings over the entire soffit area. Rectangular or triangular gable vents, often used in combination with soffit vents, are set into a wall near the peak of the roof and fastened to rafters, to vertical beams called studs and to bracing beams called headers that are part of the installation. Roof vents are set into the roof itself, between rafters, while cupola and ridge vents are set into the roof at its highest point, where the rafters meet the ridge beam.

Installing a single soffit vent. Make a cardboard template matching the part of the vent that will fit into the soffit. Locate a section of the soffit between two lookout beams—you can identify their positions by the exposed heads of the nails that fasten the soffit to the lookouts—and use the template to mark cutting lines for the vent hole. Drill a hole at the corners of the outline as starting points for a keyhole or saber saw, then cut along the lines. Screw the vent to the soffit.

Installing a fully vented soffit. For a fully vented soffit you must remove the existing soffit, which is held in place mainly by nails that are driven through it and into the lookouts, although it may also rest on a strip of molding at the top of the wall and against a fascia board at the edge of the roof. You may not have to remove the molding or the board to take the soffit out. Cut access holes between the lookouts, then pry the soffit from the lookouts with a hammer and chisel. Free the outer edge of the soffit first, so that you can swing it below the fascia board, then pull an entire soffit section off the top of the molding. Replace the section with a fully vented soffit, nailing each section to the lookouts.

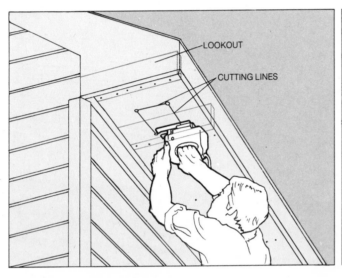

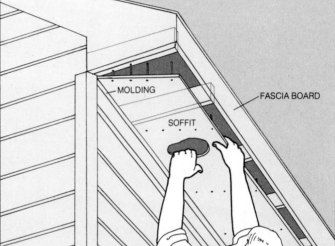

Installing a Strip Vent

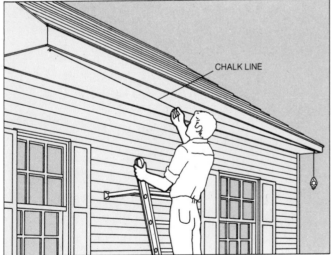

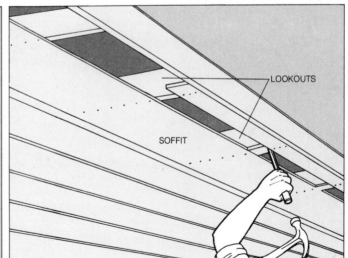

1 Marking the vent's position. At each end of the soffit, make a mark about 3 inches in from the roof edge. Snap a chalk line between the two marks as the outer cutting line for the vent. Measuring in from the chalk line, make two additional marks at a distance equal to the width of the part of the vent that will fit into the soffit. Between the marks, snap a second chalk line.

2 Cutting the vent channel. Cut along the chalk lines between lookouts. Then make cuts between the lines to remove a soffit strip, leaving only the parts nailed to the lookouts. Cut into each piece along the chalk lines and pry it loose with a chisel. Slip each vent section into the channel and nail it to the lookouts. If the lookouts prevent a good fit, chisel out enough to seat the vent.

Gable Vents

Rectangular or triangular vents in the gables at the ends of an attic are essentially exit holes for hot or moist air passing out of a house near the peak of the roof. Since a triangular vent can be located nearer the very peak of the roof, where the hottest air concentrates, it is the more efficient of the two shapes. Get a model pitched at the same angle as your roof (some are adjustable). A rectangular vent is somewhat easier to install, and many homeowners prefer it for that reason.

To install either type, cut through the siding of the house, the sheathing behind it and—probably—part of a stud. These cuts are easily made with a saber saw, and the installation of one or more 2-by-4 horizontal bracing beams called headers (Step 2, right) will leave the wall even stronger than before. Caulk with roofing cement all around the new vent to make a rain-tight seal.

3 Putting in the vent. Working outside the house, apply caulking to the outer flange of the vent and set the vent into the hole you have cut, with the vent louvers angled down. Have a helper hold the vent in place if necessary and, working inside the house, fasten the vent to the headers with nails driven through the inner flange of the vent.

If nail holes are provided in the outer flange (inset), from the outside of the house, nail the vent to the siding with aluminum or brass nails. Caulk the outer edge of the vent flange as you would caulk the edge of a door or window (page 18) but use roofing cement. Since the outer vent flange will not fit flush against clapboard siding, fill the spaces between the flange and the siding with generous amounts of roofing cement.

A Rectangular Opening

1 Cutting a vent hole. Locate the vent as close to the peak of the roof as possible, but leave enough space above the vent hole for headers (Step 2). Inside the attic, mark cutting lines on the attic wall for a rectangle ¼ inch larger than the part of the vent that will fit into the wall. Drill holes through the wall at the corners of the marked rectangle as starting points for a saber or keyhole saw, and cut through the sheathing and siding. You may have to remove a section of a stud; if so, cut away 1½ inches of the stud above and below the vent hole, to allow for headers.

2 Installing headers. Cut two pieces of 2-by-4 long enough to fit between the uncut studs at the left and right of the vent hole. These headers will make a frame for the upper and lower edges of the hole. Fasten them in position with nails driven horizontally through the uncut studs into the end of each header, and then vertically through the center of each header into the end of the cut stud above and below.

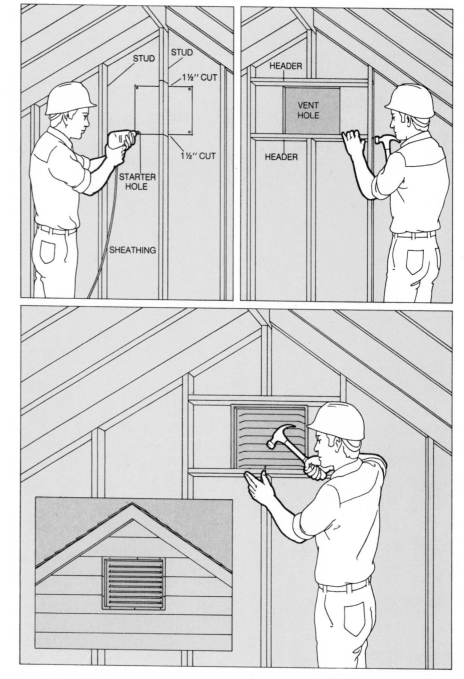

A Triangular Opening

1 **Cutting a hole.** Inside the attic, mark cutting lines to match the part of the vent that will fit through the wall; the peak of the marked triangle should be just below the bottom of the ridge beam. Drill starter holes at the corners of the triangle and use a saw to cut out the outlined hole. You will probably have to cut through at least one stud; cut away 1½ inches of the stud below the opening to allow for a 2-by-4 header.

2 **Installing a single header.** Cut a length of 2-by-4 lumber as a header between the uncut studs at the base of the vent hole. Fasten the header in position as you would the lower header for a rectangular vent (*opposite, Step 2*). Cut two more 2-by-4 lengths and attach them to the bottom edges of the rafters above the hole as shown.

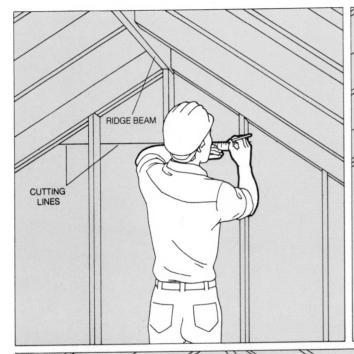

3 **Putting in the vent.** Apply roofing cement to the outer vent flange (*inset*), fit the vent into position in the wall, and nail the inner vent flange to the rafters and the header. If nail holes are provided in the outer flange, nail it to the sheathing. With the vent in place, caulk all around the edge of the outer flange with roofing cement as described for a rectangular vent (*opposite*).

Installing Roof Vents

Gable vents need a slight breeze to work well. A roof vent works even in calm weather, because it takes advantage of hot air's tendency to rise. Only a ridge vent or cupola vent *(page 58),* installed at the peak of a roof, is more efficient.

The top of a roof vent may be either round or square, but it generally covers a circular hole that provides an escape hatch for the air. A screen bars insects, and the vent top and a raised rim around the vent hole keep rain or snow from falling through into the attic. The assembly is mounted on a square metal sheet, caulked at its edges to seal the base of the hole against wind and water.

For any but the smallest attic, you will need at least two roof vents to provide the minimum venting area *(page 52).* Before cutting the vent holes through the wooden roof sheathing, you must cut away some of the shingles and roofing felt with a knife and, when the installation is complete, repair the shingles by the methods shown on pages 40-45.

1 **Rough-positioning the vent.** Set the vent assembly on the roof at the back of the house, far enough below the roof ridge to hide the vent top from a helper on the ground in front of the house. Then slide the vent horizontally along the roof to the position you want. If you are installing more than one, be sure that they will be evenly spaced. After finding a tentative position for the vent, measure the distances from the center of the vent assembly to the ridge and the nearest roof edge. Subtract the distance of any overhang from the latter measurement.

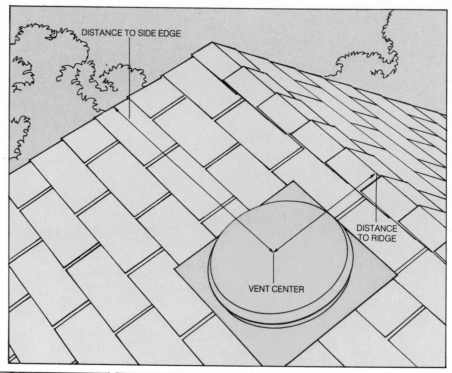

2 **Fixing the final position.** Inside the attic, use the measurements from Step 1 to locate the tentative position you have chosen for the vent. In its final position, the vent hole must be centered exactly between two rafters. Find the center point closest to the tentative position and drive a nail through the roof to mark it. The procedure should change the vent position that was selected in Step 1 by only a few inches.

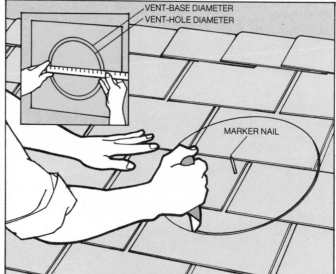

3 **Clearing the vent area.** Locate the marker nail on the outside of the roof. Measure the diameter of the base of the vent housing *(inset)* and, using the marker nail as a center point, scribe a circle of this diameter into the shingles. Remove the shingles, roofing felt and nails within the circle.

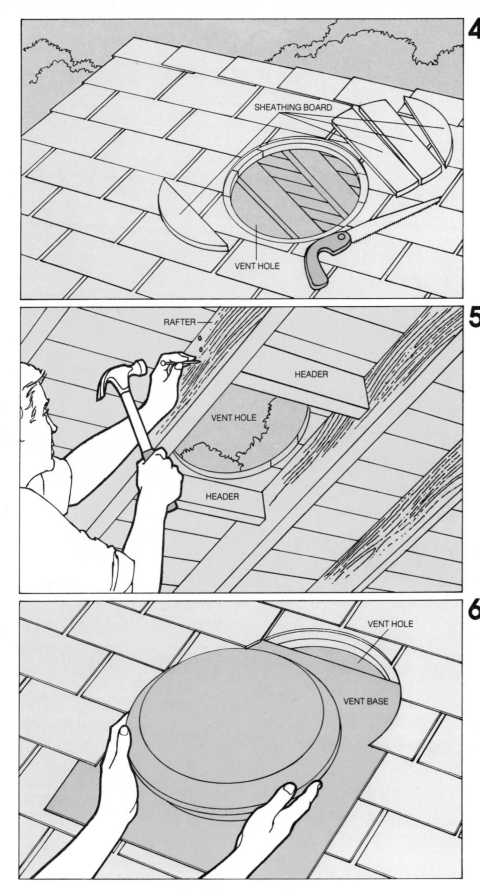

4 **Cutting the vent hole.** Measure the inside diameter of the vent hole and scribe a circle of this diameter within the area cleared in Step 3. Cut away the sheathing boards inside the circle with a saber or keyhole saw. The hole should have a slightly larger circle of cleared sheathing around it.

5 **Putting in headers.** Cut two headers from 2-by-4 lumber long enough to fit between the rafters to the left and right of the vent hole. Fasten the headers above and below the hole by nailing through the rafters into the ends of the headers.

6 **Installing the vent assembly.** Apply caulking to the underside of the vent base, then slide it up under the loosened shingles around the vent hole and into position over the hole; if the nails holding the surrounding shingles interfere, remove them (*page 42*). Have a helper in the attic check to be sure that the inside of the vent is centered over the vent hole in the roof. Fasten the base to the roof with 1½-inch roofing nails driven through the mounting holes. Apply additional caulking at the exposed bottom edge of the base and repair the loose shingles around the vent by the methods shown on pages 40-45.

Peak Vents for Best Air Flow

The hottest, dampest air in the attic collects at the highest point under the roof, and the best way to get rid of it is to install a vent in the roof's peak. Two vents are made for this purpose: ridge vents *(below),* which run the length of the roof peak, and cupola vents *(right),* which are inside a decorative cupola installed at the center of the roof peak. The ridge vent is more efficient because it has an outlet along the entire roof instead of only at one point, and it also operates more effectively in still air. Unlike the cupola vent, a ridge vent is not camouflaged by a decorative exterior, but its low profile makes it relatively unobtrusive. When installed with soffit vents, both ridge and cupola vents are more efficient than any other combination.

Because of their location, ridge and cupola vents are more difficult to install than soffit, gable or roof vents—the job is often left to a professional. For both, roof shingles must be removed and sheathing cut; a cupola vent may also require that a piece be cut from the ridge beam if the vent has a central duct. This operation seems more drastic than it really is, for the ridge beam is not critical to the structural strength of the house—the sheathing holds everything together.

The cupola vent. A short duct capped with a little roof of its own, this vent fits into a hole cut through the sheathing and, in some cases, the ridge beam. If you must remove part of a ridge beam, headers at the sides of the vent hole replace the missing section, and the central duct is fastened to the headers. Outside the roof, the bottom edge of the cupola has a flange of flashing that fits under the surrounding shingles and is caulked with roofing cement.

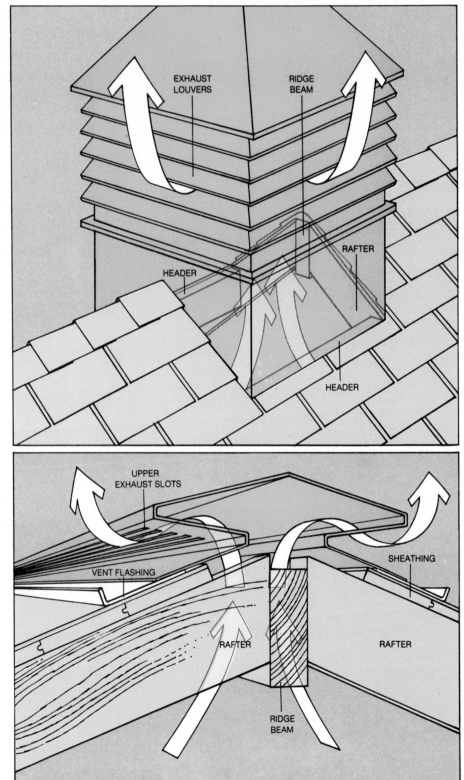

The ridge vent. A continuous opening cut through sheathing along the roof peak allows hot air in the attic to rise into the vent and leave through the upper exhaust slots. To install the vent, the shingles along the roof ridge and the roofing felt beneath them are removed and an inch of sheathing on either side of the roof peak is cut away. The vent is then nailed over the hole along the roof peak through its flashing and sealed with roofing cement.

Airing a Dank Basement

Even after you have eliminated leaks and seepage *(pages 30-36),* you may still have moisture in the basement or the crawl space. If it is unventilated and unheated —and especially if it has a dirt floor —moisture condenses on joists and the undersides of floorboards, and spreads upward inside the house walls. Covering a dirt floor with a vapor barrier *(page 92)* is the essential first step. But if your basement or crawl space lacks ventilation, also install ventilators. With a vapor barrier on the floor, most experts recommend one ventilator for every 300 or so square feet of floor area.

Install the ventilators near the top of the foundation walls and close to the corner, but not right next to it. At a minimum there should be two ventilators in opposite walls. In the rare instances when more than two are needed, distribute them equally in all the walls.

In a cold climate you will need to insulate the underside of the first floor *(page 90)* if it has not already been done. Outside air in winter is as much as five times drier than in summer, so you can reduce air circulation and still get rid of unwanted moisture by partially closing ventilators—but leave some opening.

Mortaring the ventilator. With chisel and hammer make an opening in the foundation wall slightly larger than the ventilator. If you expose block cores, pack them with paper to within an inch of the surface and fill them the rest of the way with mortar. Let it cure for 24 hours. Halfway back and on the bottom of the opening, lay a bead of mortar the width of the ventilator and ¾ inch high. Place the ventilator on the mortar and then pack mortar around the other edges of the ventilator with a mason's tool, called a joint filler, or with a blunt kitchen knife.

Making a coping. So that rain water does not accumulate on the sill outside or inside the ventilator, build up a coping, or sloping surface, on both sides of the ventilator. Trowel mortar up to the bottom of the ventilator and then slant it toward the edge of the foundation wall. Place damp rags on the mortar to cure it for 24 hours.

Expelling Moisture from Kitchen, Bath and Laundry

The unpowered vents in an attic *(pages 52-58)* can solve only a part of a family's venting problems: cooking, bathing and washing clothes for a family of four can release as much as 3 gallons of water a day into the house, in the form of vapor. In a poorly insulated house a great deal of moisture escapes harmlessly through walls and cracks. But when you tighten your home against the weather, you seal off these escape routes. The moisture accumulates in the air, and it can cause peeling paint, sticky drawers and mildew. To solve the problem, force water vapor out of the house by installing exhaust fans in rooms where it is generated: kitchen, bathroom and laundry.

In an existing house, the easiest installation for the kitchen is a through-wall fan with a built-in switch *(below)*. For the bathroom build a smaller fan into the ceiling *(pages 64-65)*. In the laundry you need only vent the drier directly outdoors with a drier vent kit *(pages 66-67)*.

A fan should change the air in a kitchen every four minutes, in a bathroom every seven and a half minutes. To find the size fan you need, determine the cubic feet of space in the room, then divide that figure by 4 for a kitchen, 7.5 for a bathroom. The result is the CFM rating you need—the capacity of the fan in cubic feet of air moved each minute. A second rating indicates a fan's sound output in units called sones. Compare the sone ratings of different models in your CFM range and choose the lowest for quiet operation.

Installing a kitchen exhaust fan in most houses takes only a few hours, although breaking through and patching a brick wall is more involved. The only special tools you are likely to need are the fish tapes to pull the wires for the fan motor through the wall. You will also need three-wire cable and two cable connectors to wire the fan to the house circuit.

Locate a kitchen fan in an outside wall, 30 inches or more above the surface of the range. If the range is placed against an inside wall, use the nearest outside wall. Since a kitchen fan pulls particles of cooking grease along with the heat and moisture it exhausts, it is a good idea to place a grease filter between the fan grille and the motor; otherwise grease may damage the motor.

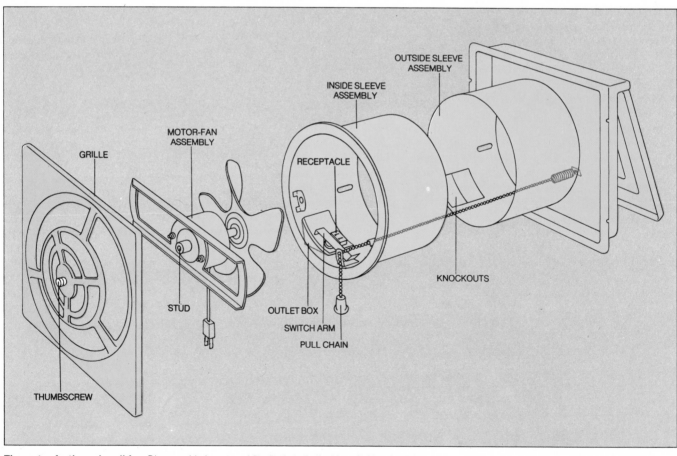

The parts of a through-wall fan. Disassembled for installation, the components in this drawing fit into a hole cut through the wall. The outside sleeve assembly is fastened to the wall from outdoors; the inside sleeve assembly slides into it and fits flush to the inside wall. Knockouts can be removed to shorten the sleeve assemblies for different wall thicknesses. Wires from a house electrical circuit attach to corresponding wires inside the outlet box, and the fan motor plugs into a receptacle in the box cover. The pull chain opens and closes the shutter and operates the switch arm, turning the fan on when the shutter is open, off when it is closed. A grille, held by a thumbscrew, fits over a motor-bracket stud.

An Exhaust Fan in a Wall

1 **Cutting the inside hole.** Drill a ½-inch hole through the wall at the point you have chosen for the center of the fan, and probe inside the wall with a wire for the studs on either side. The fan opening must be at least 2 inches from the studs; if it is not, move the center hole. Make a template matching the inner sleeve opening, and use it to mark a circle on the wall. Drill ½-inch starter holes at the 3, 6 and 9 o'clock positions on the circle, and cut out the opening with a saber or keyhole saw. If necessary, remove enough insulation to accommodate the inner sleeve.

If your walls consist of cinder block or clay tile, use a masonry bit to drill the test hole; hollow out the inside with a cold chisel and hammer.

2 **Cutting the outside hole.** Insert the inner sleeve into the hole you have cut out and push the template to the far end of the sleeve. Drill a ½-inch hole through the center of the template and on through the outside wall. Remove the inside sleeve and the template. Outside the house, center the template over the drilled hole and use it to mark a circle around the template. Drill starter holes and saw an opening as in Step 1, making the cut just outside the marked line.

If the outside wall is stucco, score the circle with a utility knife and use a metal-cutting blade in your saber saw. If it is a brick wall, remove mortar and take out all the bricks within the circle and any that have the circle mark running through them. Cut each brick separately along the mark with a mason's chisel. Mortar the cut pieces into place around the outside of the circle.

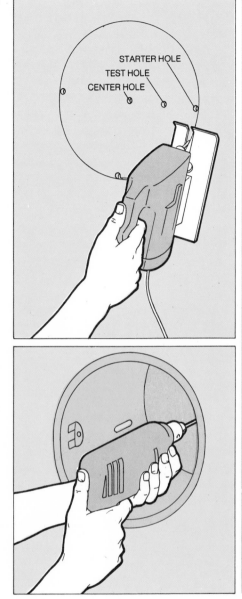

STARTER HOLE
TEST HOLE
CENTER HOLE

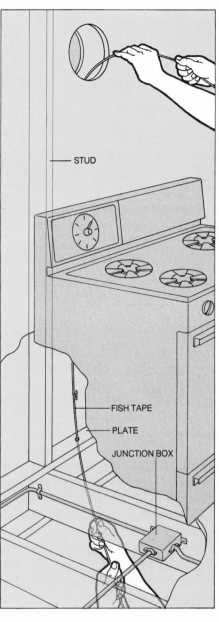

STUD

FISH TAPE

PLATE

JUNCTION BOX

3 **Bringing wiring to the fan.** Run a three-wire cable to the fan hole from a junction box. The most likely place to find a box is in the basement ceiling. To locate the best path for the cable from the basement, look for utility lines coming up through the floor. If you do not find any, drill a small hole in the floor beneath the fan opening. From the basement, drill a ¾-inch hole up through the plate near this locator hole. Lower the end of a fish tape through the fan opening and have a helper push another fish tape up through the hole in the plate. Hook them together inside the wall and draw the hooks into the basement. Disconnect the hooks, tape the end of the cable to the upper hook, and pull the cable up and through the fan opening. Tape it temporarily to the wall.

4 Mounting the outside sleeve. Tape the shutter closed to keep it out of the way while you are working. Adjust the depth of the fan sleeves, if necessary, by removing one or more knockouts in the outside sleeve and slide the sleeve into the outside wall. Align the flanges with the siding above and below, and screw them to the wall. Caulk around the edges of the flanges.

5 Attaching cable to the outlet box. Working inside the house, remove the outlet box from the inside sleeve, and run the cable through the box hole. Slide the sleeve into the fan opening and screw it to the outside sleeve. Remove a knockout from the outlet box and screw a cable connector into the knockout hole. Run the end of the cable through the connector and tighten the clamp. Refasten the outlet box.

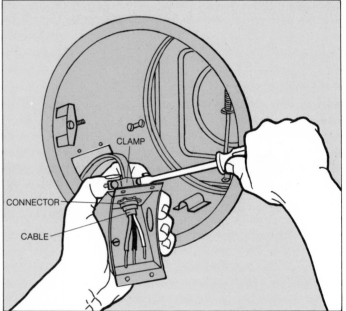

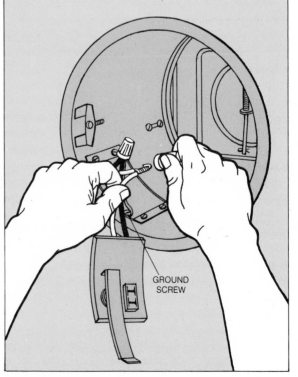

6 Connecting the wires. Twist the stranded black wire from the outlet-box cover around the solid black wire of the house cable, then bend the end of the solid wire back upon itself and twist a wire cap down over the insulation. Connect the white wires in the same way. Secure the bare copper wire of the house cable to the green ground screw in the outlet box. Screw the outlet-box cover back into place.

7 Attaching the pull chain. Align the screw hole of the chain-catch bracket with the corresponding hole in the bottom of the inside sleeve, and fasten the bracket in place. Hook the spring at one end of the chain into the bracket at the far end of the shutter, then run it through the tunnel-like guard at the bottom of the sleeve, over the switch arm and through the chain-catch bracket. Outside the house, remove the tape from the shutter. With the shutter open, cut the chain to a convenient length and attach the pendant to its end.

8 Installing the motor-fan assembly. With the motor cord and plug facing down, fit the keyholes of the motor bracket over the screws in the small tabs at the sides of the inside sleeve. Turn the bracket to fit the screws into the narrow ends of the keyholes; tighten the screws. Turn the blades manually to make sure nothing obstructs them.

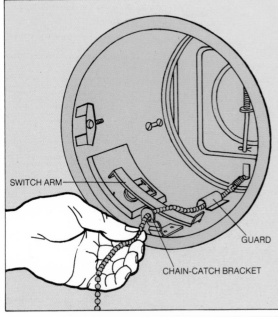

SWITCH ARM

GUARD

CHAIN-CATCH BRACKET

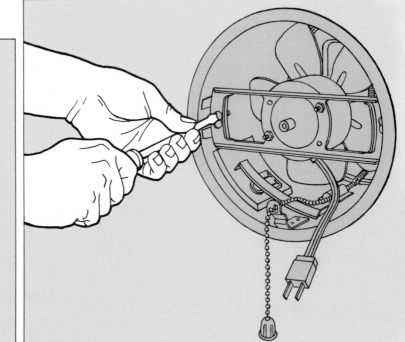

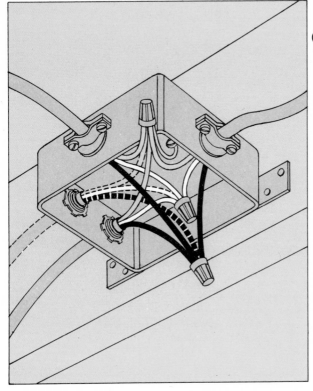

9 Connecting wires at the junction box. Because the wires of several circuits may run through a single junction box, turn off all the house circuits at the fuse or circuit-breaker panel before connecting the new cable. Then open the junction box and remove the wire caps. Test to be sure the power is off; touch one prong of a voltage tester to the metal of the box and the other prong to each of the wires in the box. The bulb of the tester should not light if the power is off.

Remove a knockout from the box, install a cable connector in the knockout hole and run the end of the new cable through the connector; tighten the clamp to hold the cable firm. Join the new wires, shown here as broken lines, to wires in the box—black to black, white to white, and the copper ground wire to all the other ground wires. If necessary, replace wire caps with larger ones. Restore power to the circuits, plug in the fan and switch it on to check its operation.

If you are using a grease filter, place it over the motor bracket; set the grille into position and run the pull chain through both the filter and the grille. Screw the grille thumbscrew into the motor-bracket stud until the grille is flush to the wall.

An Exhaust Fan in a Ceiling

For a fan intended to remove warm, moist air, the best location is the ceiling, and the moderate-capacity fans that are sufficient for bathrooms are small enough to fit inside a standard ceiling space. Such a fan needs a duct to exhaust outdoors. For an upstairs bathroom, the duct generally runs straight up through attic and roof. If the fan is in an interior room on the first floor of a two-story house, you simply need more ducting and an improvised method for getting it to the outside —inside a built-in cabinet, through a closet or if necessary along a corner where the duct can be concealed with a wallboard enclosure. If the bathroom, upstairs or down, has an exterior wall, you can eliminate ductwork by installing a through-the-wall kitchen-type fan using the instructions on pages 60-63.

Be certain to get a fan that is the correct size for your bathroom, using the formula on page 60. If the exhaust duct will need an elbow, or bend, in it, buy a fan with the next higher CFM rating.

To estimate how much ducting you will need, measure the route from fan to roof, allow for bends and add 2 inches for the roof thickness and 2 inches to extend above the roof. You also will need a roof cap to fit the duct, roofing cement to install it, plus No. 12 electrical cable and fittings to wire the fan.

The fan is connected to the bathroom light so that it operates whenever the light is switched on. If the light fixture is in the ceiling and you can reach it from the attic, all you need do is connect the wires. If not, you will need cable fish tapes (page 61) to pull the new wiring inside the walls from fan to light fixture.

1 **Opening the attic floor.** Drill a ⅛-inch test hole through the bathroom ceiling where you want the fan. If the bit does not go through quickly, it has hit a joist. Fill the hole with spackling compound and drill another test hole 2 inches away. If the attic is unfloored, proceed to Step 2. If the attic is floored, enlarge the hole with a ¾-inch bit, then, using an extension and a ⅛-inch bit, drill through the attic floor. If the attic floor is insulated, run coat-hanger wire up through the test hole to mark the spot. The test hole marks the center of the fan. Use it to mark an opening in the floor that will extend between the two joists adjacent to the hole and be large enough to accommodate the fan housing and its duct connection. Cut the floor with a keyhole or saber saw and remove insulation if there is any.

2 **Mounting the fan housing.** Detach the housing from the grille and the fan-motor assembly. Working from the attic, center the housing over the locator hole and against the joist nearest the hole. Mark a line on the ceiling around the lip that will extend through the ceiling and cut a hole along the line. Remove a knockout from the fan outlet box and install a cable connector in the box. Lower the housing along the joist until the lip is flush with the ceiling, then screw it to the joist.

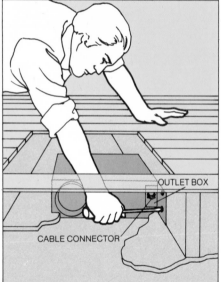

OUTLET BOX

CABLE CONNECTOR

3 **Framing the opening.** To support the flooring you will replace after installing the fan, nail 2-by-4s along the joists at the opening. For additional support around the opening, toenail 2-by-4s around it. The tops of these pieces must be flush with the tops of the joists.

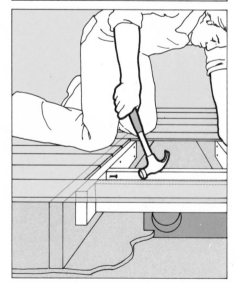

4 **Installing the duct and roof cap.** Hold a piece of duct against the roof underside at the point where the duct will go through. Angle the duct if necessary to avoid obstructions and to bring it to a convenient point on the roof. Mark around the duct end and drive a nail through the center of the marked area. Outside, on the roof, center a piece of duct over the protruding nail and use a linoleum knife to mark a line around the duct. Remove shingle, roofing felt and nails inside the circle as for a roof vent *(pages 56-57)*. Saw through the roof sheathing, following the circle. Slide the cap's built-in flashing under the shingles around the hole, and cut away any portion of shingle that prevents the roof-cap hood from fitting over the hole. Remove the roof cap and set it aside.

Run the ducting from the fan housing through the hole in the roof. Seal connections in the duct with duct tape, and cut off the duct ½ inch above the roof surface at an angle that conforms to the roof. Thinly coat the underside of the roof-cap flashing with roofing cement and press it into place. Apply roofing cement to the undersides of shingles that overlap the flashing.

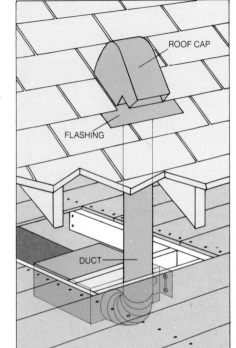

ROOF CAP

FLASHING

DUCT

5 **Wiring and mounting the fan.** Working from the attic, run No. 12 cable through the connector you installed in Step 2 and tighten the clamp on the cable. Working from the bathroom side, remove the fan's outlet-box cover and attach the wires—black to black, white to white, and the bare copper wire to the green screw terminal—as described in Step 6 on page 62. Replace the outlet-box cover and mount the motor-fan assembly in the housing, making sure to center the thumbscrew that will hold the grille in place.

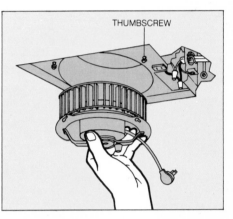

THUMBSCREW

Wiring the Fan to a Light Fixture

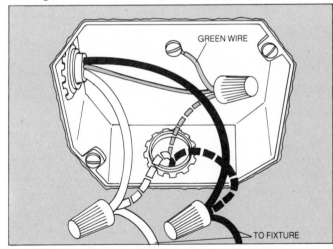

GREEN WIRE

TO FIXTURE

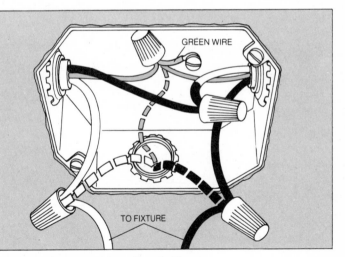

GREEN WIRE

TO FIXTURE

Connections for a middle-of-the-run switch. At the fuse box or circuit-breaker panel, turn off the power to the bathroom light. Remove the light fixture and disconnect its wiring. Check with a voltage tester to make sure the power is off—one prong of the tester against the metal of the box and the other against each wire in the box; the bulb of the tester should not light. The drawing above shows one wiring arrangement you are likely to make; the other common arrangement is at right. If only one cable—from the switch—enters the box, take out the box that holds the light fixture's wiring and bring the new cable to the fixture, using fish tapes as in Step 3, page 61. Then follow the instructions in Step 9, page 63, to connect the new wires to those in the box. New wires are indicated by broken lines.

Connections for a switch loop. If you find two cables already entering the light fixture, the light is part of a switch loop. Both wires in the cable leading to and from the switch are hot—the white wire should be recoded black with black markings on its end. To be sure you are connecting the fan to the wire that brings power to the box, have a helper turn on the power while you carefully hold one prong of a voltage tester against a black wire and the other against the metal of the box—the bulb will light when the probe is touched to the wire carrying current. Turn off the power and then connect wires as indicated by the broken lines in the drawing above.

A Clothes Drier Exhaust Duct

A clothes drier dumps 8 or 9 pounds of vaporized water into a laundry room with every average load—enough moisture to cause damage in most homes. To discharge this exhaust outdoors, you hook up a special clothes-drier vent before you set the drier into its permanent position. Such vents come in kits that consist of a flexible plastic duct, clamps and a hood vent pipe. Make sure you get one the right size to fit your drier's exhaust outlets, and get a vent pipe to suit the installation you plan.

Driers can be vented through a window *(right),* with a 3-inch-long pipe or through a wall *(opposite),* with a 12-inch-long pipe. The method you choose will depend on the design and construction of your house as well as where you put the clothes drier. The window vent is easiest to install. Simply replace one pane of glass with a vent plate bored to hold the pipe. Prebored vent plates are available in transparent plastic or in aluminum. However, you can make your own out of a scrap of ¼-inch exterior plywood and then paint it the same color as the window frame.

If you do not have a convenient window, or if your windows are close to plants that the exhaust would parch, you will need a wall vent. This requires making a large hole through the foundation if it is made of cinder block, or through the siding and header joist if the foundation is poured concrete. Either job is fairly simple with an electric drill.

For efficient venting, the duct should always be as short and straight as possible. Although a plastic duct can bend to snake around pipes or joists, and extra units may be added for stretches of more than the kit's usual 20 feet, loops and long distances slow down the air flow and may cause the duct to clog with lint.

PLASTIC VENT PLATE

VENT PIPE

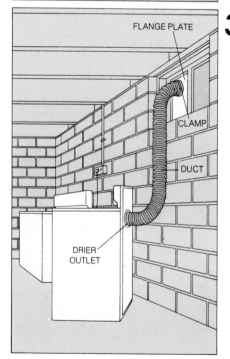

FLANGE PLATE

CLAMP

DUCT

DRIER OUTLET

Installing a Vent in a Window

1 Attaching the vent plate. Chisel out the putty around one pane of glass, pry out the glazing points and remove the pane. Wearing goggles, use a hacksaw to cut the vent plate to fit the window opening. Then, working from outside the house, set the plate into the opening. Anchor the plate with glazing points and seal the edges with glazing compound. Nail the window shut so that it cannot be opened accidentally.

To make a plywood vent plate, use the pipe as a template for drawing a circle of the required size on the wood. Cut out the circle with a keyhole saw, then trim the plywood to fit the window opening. Follow the procedures above for removing the glass and installing the wooden plate.

2 Inserting the vent pipe. Slide off the flange plate from the back of a 3-inch-long vent pipe. Working from outside the house, push the pipe through the hole in the vent plate until the back of the hood is flush with the plate.

3 Attaching the duct. From inside the house, slip the flange plate over the back of the pipe and press it firmly against the vent plate. Place a clamp on one end of the duct, then fit the duct over the pipe and anchor it by tightening the clamp. Move the drier to its permanent place and extend the duct to the exhaust outlet on the drier. Use scissors or wire cutters to cut off excess duct. Slide a clamp around the loose end of the duct, slip the duct over the drier exhaust outlet and tighten the clamp.

To prevent the duct from stretching or sagging, anchor it with strings tied to nails in the wall or ceiling joists, or with perforated metal straps held in shape by nuts and bolts and nailed in place.

Installing a Vent in Masonry

1 Making the opening. Locate the exhaust opening close to the drier but away from pipes and shrubs, and outline it with masking tape, indoors and out, in a circle the same diameter as the vent pipe. Wearing goggles, use a ½-inch masonry bit in an electric drill to bore several holes in the circle from outside, penetrating to the hollow core. Knock out the material between the holes with a cold chisel and hammer. Chip away the edges of the opening until it is large enough for the pipe. Then bore and chisel out the opening on the inside of the block.

2 Sealing the vent pipe. Spread a 1-inch band of mortar around the exterior opening in the cinder block. Slide the interior flange plate off a 12-inch-long vent pipe and spread mortar around the pipe behind the hood. Push the pipe into the opening, pressing the hood in firmly to squeeze out the excess mortar; wipe it off. Working inside the house, clean away any mortar inside the pipe. Spread mortar around the interior opening in the block, then slip the flange onto the pipe and press it on firmly. Wipe up the excess. Attach the duct to the pipe and drier *(opposite, bottom)*.

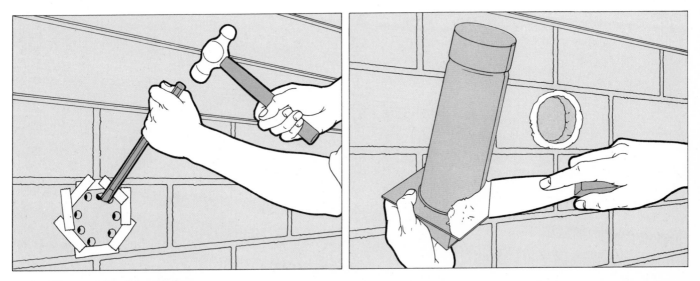

Installing a Vent in Siding

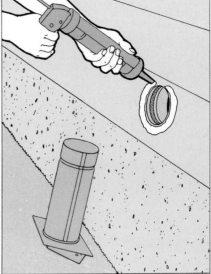

1 Cutting the opening. Use the pipe as a template to draw a circle on the siding over the header joist but between the ceiling joists. Then cut the opening through the siding, through the sheathing and through the header joist. As you saw through each layer, remove the material so you can get at the next layer easily. The hole can be cut by drilling a starter hole and using a keyhole saw for wood, or a saber saw with a metal-cutting blade for aluminum or asbestos siding. A circle cutter in a ⅜- or ½-inch electric drill is faster, but practice using it before you try it on the wall.

2 Sealing the pipe. To weatherproof the opening, seal it all around inside and outside with butyl or silicone caulk applied the same way as mortar in a cinder-block installation *(top, right)*.

3

Shielding against Cold and Heat

Forms of insulation. Though they all have the same function—to block the flow of heat out of or into a house—these insulation materials come in a bewildering variety of forms. Clockwise from the top are three fiber batts, one without a vapor barrier, the others with barriers of paper and foil; a glob of plastic foam; and heaps of vermiculite, perlite and cellulose loose insulation. Rigid foamed plastic boards are shown in the center.

According to a reliable estimate, over 40 million homes in the United States are inadequately protected against winter and summer weather. These homes are poorly caulked or weather-stripped, lack tight-fitting storm doors and windows or, most important, have poor insulation in their ceilings, walls and floors. If they were effectively protected, the savings would come to nearly a fifth of the money spent for home heating and cooling every year.

Because poor insulation accounts for the greatest waste of fuel, this chapter tells how to improve the insulation you already have and how to install it in areas that have none. In each case, the object is the same: to block the flow of heat into or out of the house. Heat always flows from an area of higher temperature to one of lower, just as water flows from a high point to a lower one. Some materials are good conductors of the flow of heat—the aluminum or copper bottom of a pan, for instance, quickly passes heat from the flame below to the food above. Others, like the asbestos pad that keeps the hot pan from scorching a countertop, resist the flow.

Wood, sheet glass, metal and solid masonry—the materials used to build a house—are generally poor resisters of heat flow. Certain natural and man-made insulating materials, however, resist it superbly. A modern fiberglass blanket only 6 inches thick blocks the flow of heat as effectively as 8 feet of solid brick wall. Unfortunately, many homes do not take advantage of such powerful insulators. Older houses, built when fuel costs were comparatively low, saved on insulation but waste electricity, oil or gas. To make them economical today, they need a systematic program of analysis and installation.

First compare the insulation you have with the insulation you need. Next check to see that your insulation is at the right level—first at the attic or roof, where warm rising air causes the greatest heat loss, then at exterior walls, and finally in the basement or crawl space under the house. The cost of rectifying insulation deficiencies can usually be recovered in fuel savings within four years—sometimes in as little as two—and the result is a house that is not only less expensive to maintain but more comfortable in all weathers.

Windows and doors call for a different treatment. They cannot be insulated in the usual way, but they do form paths of heat loss in winter and unwanted heat gain in summer. Storm windows or doors —essentially double windows or doors, with a layer of insulating air trapped by a sheet of glass or plastic—can cut these losses and gains by as much as half. And for the special problem of summer glare and heat, there is an old-fashioned solution with some new-fangled improvements—awnings, now often made of plastic or aluminum, or plastic window films that serve the same purpose.

A Guide to the Complexities of Insulation

All home insulating materials have certain features in common. Light for their bulk, they are fluffy or foamy—even rigid insulation boards have the feel of congealed foam. They have these qualities because they consist mainly of tiny pockets of trapped air.

The air pockets resist the flow of heat out of or into a house. Heating engineers rate the resistance on a scale of R-values, based on the amount of heat that will pass through a square foot of a material in one hour when the temperature on one side is 1° higher than on the other. The R-value depends on both the composition and thickness of the material (chart, below).

By far the most common material used for insulation consists of fibers—fibers of glass; rock-wool fibers, made by blowing steam through molten rock; and cellulose, or plant fibers. There are two common ways of packaging this material: in long rolls that are called blankets, or precut flexible rectangles called batts (opposite, top).

Fibers can also be used as loose-fill insulation, poured or blown onto attic floors or into hollow walls. Besides fibers, loose fill may consist of pellets or granules, usually made of vermiculite (a form of mica) or perlite (volcanic ash).

The remaining insulating materials are man-made synthetics. One type comes in rigid boards or sheets and is widely used to insulate masonry walls. Another, called foamed-in-place, consists of a plastic foam that flows around obstructions to fill a space completely, then hardens to a rigid mass.

By blocking heat flow, insulation solves one problem but introduces another. It increases the temperature difference between inside and outside wall surfaces. And temperature determines how much vapor air can hold; moisture that is vapor at the interior temperature turns to liquid at the lower exterior temperature. The water makes insulation worthless, and damages paint and wood.

The solution to the problem is a vapor barrier—a layer of impervious material that prevents water vapor from reaching a section cold enough to make it condense. Most blankets and batts are sold with a vapor barrier already installed. With loose fill you can install a separate barrier or cover the interior of an insulated wall with oil-base enamel paint and a top coat of alkyd paint.

Types of Insulation

Material	Approximate R-value per inch of thickness	Form	Advantages	Disadvantages
Vermiculite	2.08	Loose fill	Especially suitable for the spaces in hollow-core blocks	Low insulation efficiency; moisture-absorbent
Perlite	2.70	Loose fill	Easily poured into hollow spaces	Comparable to vermiculite
Fiberglass	3.33	Blankets, batts, loose fill	Relatively inexpensive; fire-resistant	Particles can irritate skin; gives off odor when damp
Rock wool	3.33	Blankets, batts, loose fill	Comparable to fiberglass	Particles can irritate skin
Polystyrene	3.45	Rigid boards	Moisture-resistant; useful for below-grade floors and exterior walls	Highly combustible; easily dented
Cellulose	3.70	Blankets, batts, loose fill	Fine consistency permits loose-fill installation through small access holes; does not irritate skin	Flammable unless chemically treated
Urethane	5.30	Foamed-in-place	Highest insulation efficiency	Requires professional installation; gives off noxious gases if ignited

Comparing insulation materials. Although insulation is marketed under a bewildering variety of trade names, almost all of it uses one of the basic materials listed by their generic names on this chart. Fiberglass and rock wool account for more than 90 per cent of all insulation sold in the United States and Canada, but the others have distinctive forms or properties, listed in the last three columns, that make them preferable to fibers in some applications.

The materials are ranked in an ascending order of resistance to heat flow, or R-value. The R numbers, given here as R-value per inch, cannot be simply added or multiplied for greater thicknesses—a glass fiber batt 6 inches thick, for example, does not have exactly six times the R-value of a 1-inch batt. The exact rating, however, is printed on all blankets, batts and boards (the 6-inch fiber batt will be rated R-19—the value recommended for exterior walls in most of the United States and Canada). When you buy loose fill, look for bags that indicate the R-value of the insulation at different thicknesses.

How Insulation Is Packaged

Blankets. These rolls of insulation are sold in thicknesses of 1 to 7 inches, lengths of 16 to 64 feet, and widths designed to fit snugly between standard stud spacings. Blankets usually have thin marginal strips, called flanges, for stapling, and a vapor barrier of paper or foil, but they also come without a barrier. Blankets are difficult to cut and are best for long runs of unobstructed space: between floor joists in an unfinished attic or between rafters in a roof.

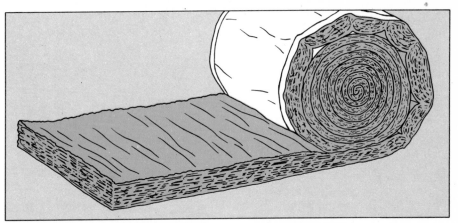

Batts. These are simply short blankets, cut into uniform lengths of 4 or 8 feet for easier handling—the 8-foot length fills the space between studs in a standard wall; an 8-foot batt plus a 4-foot one completes a common joist run of 12 feet. Batts without attached vapor barriers can be squeezed between joints without fasteners.

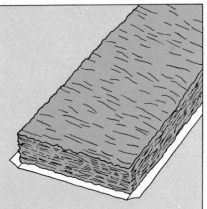

How a Vapor Barrier Works

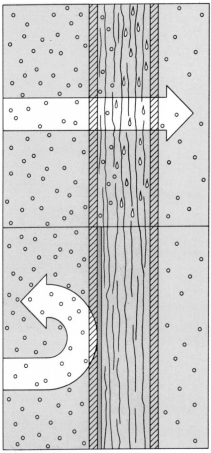

Rigid boards. Constructed from lightweight plastic foam, rigid insulation is supplied in sizes from 8-inch squares to 4-by-12-foot sheets. They provide relatively high insulation in thicknesses of ½ to 1 inch, and are often used as sheathing beneath aluminum or plastic siding. Because the plastic boards are flammable, they should not be left exposed or covered with wood paneling—on a basement wall, for example—but should be protected with gypsum wallboard, which resists fire.

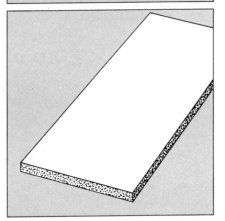

Loose fill. This type is easy to spread into open, flat spaces, such as unfloored attics, or to blow inside covered walls and floors through access holes. But it requires a separate vapor barrier, and unlike other forms of insulation, it settles, especially in walls or sloping areas. This can result in a loss of heat resistance over the years unless the fill is replenished occasionally.

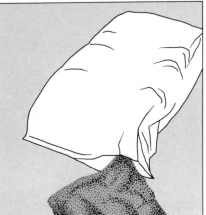

How a vapor barrier works. In winter, when the interior temperature of an insulated building is much higher than that of the air outside, warm, moist interior air releases its moisture as it passes through the insulation *(top)*, condensing into water inside the insulation and on the cold inner surface of the exterior wall.

A vapor barrier of aluminum foil, heavy plastic sheeting or waterproof paint *(bottom)* prevents water vapor from passing beyond the interior surface of the insulation—it never reaches a cold region and cannot condense.

Where to Insulate a House

Houses come in an infinitude of shapes and sizes, but all of them incorporate some of the elements of the dwelling at right. Using this drawing as a guide, make a check list of the walls, ceilings and floors that should be insulated in your own home to reduce heating and air-conditioning bills.

The overall rule for insulating a house is simple: insulation should be present at any surface separating living spaces from unheated areas, since that is where heat loss occurs—and also where the sun's heat can make unwelcome entry in the summer. All exterior walls should be insulated, not neglecting any wall of a split-level house that rises above an adjacent roof. Any wall between a heated room and an unheated area such as a garage, utility room or open porch also demands insulation, as do floors separating living spaces from such unheated areas. And do not overlook the overhanging portion of a room cantilevered out from the rest of the house.

If the house has an unheated cellar or crawl space, the floors above must be insulated. In the case of a finished basement, the below-ground walls require insulation. Similarly, the floor of an unheated attic calls for insulation, whereas a finished room in a heated attic must have an insulated ceiling and knee walls as well as protection for the ceilings and walls of all dormers.

Where insulation goes. Because heated air rises and is lost through the roof, the most critical insulation sites in this house are the floor of the unfinished attic (*far right*) and the roof above the finished attic (*right*). To complete the envelope protecting the heated interior from the unheated exterior, the exterior walls and foundation should be protected. Then come the ceilings of the unheated basement, garage and crawl space. Not to be neglected are such heat escape routes as dormers and overhangs, which should be blanketed with insulation.

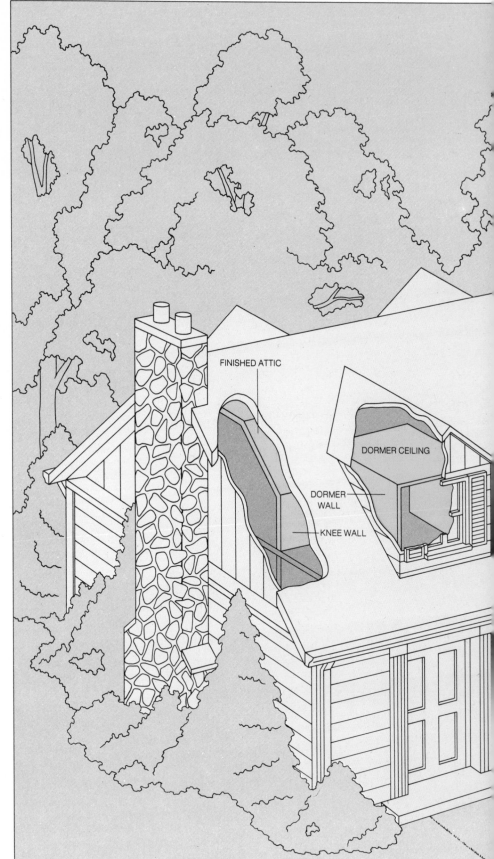

FINISHED ATTIC

DORMER CEILING

DORMER WALL

KNEE WALL

UNFINISHED ATTIC FLOOR

OVERHANG

UNHEATED GARAGE

CRAWL SPACE

FINISHED BASEMENT

How Much Insulation Do You Have?

Before you can estimate how much additional insulation your house needs you must find out how much and what kind it already has. A good place to begin your survey is in unfinished areas such as attics, basements, crawl spaces and garages. If there is insulation in these areas it will be visible between joists, beams and studs; its thickness can be readily measured with a ruler.

Insulation inside finished walls can often be checked through existing openings. The most convenient are those for switches and receptacles (below). If the wall has no outlets, look for less obvious openings. Remove the louvers of forced-air ducts and peek along the edge of the duct, or pry off a section of baseboard and chisel a small peephole through the wallboard; the hole will be concealed when the baseboard is replaced. As a last resort, drill or chisel a small opening directly into the wall; you can easily reseal the opening afterward.

Another important area of hidden insulation is the flooring of a finished attic. If the boards are simply butted alongside each other, you can pry one up for a look underneath it (opposite). Tongue-and-groove boards are difficult to separate; instead, drill a small hole through one of the boards and the subflooring underneath, then use a pencil to measure the thickness of the underlying insulation (opposite, far right).

To measure the thickness of insulation through an opening on the heated side of a wall or floor, you may have to make a fairly large tear in the vapor barrier. You can patch it with duct tape, metal foil or plastic sheeting before resealing the wall. If a check at an outlet box shows that the insulation in your wall is in the form of a blanket or batt, do not open a large tear for measurement purposes at that point; batts and blankets are usually compressed where they pass over and around electrical outlet boxes, so that any measurement is likely to be misleading. If you think the insulation does not fill the 3½-inch depth of most wood-frame walls, you will have to open a hole in the wallboard or plaster to verify your suspicion.

Once you know the thickness and type of your existing insulation, you can estimate its approximate R-value by mul-

tiplying the thickness in inches by the R-value per inch as shown in the table on page 70. For example, if you find that you have about 3½ inches of fiberglass, multiply 3.5 by 3.33—the R-value of an inch of fiberglass—for a total R-value between R-11 and R-12. If you find that the stud cavities are filled with perlite loose fill, the R-value is 3.5 times 2.70, or between R-9 and R-10; similarly, 3½ inches of urethane foam translates into an R-value between R-7 and R-8. Once you have determined the R-value of your existing insulation, you will be able to calculate how much you must add to reach the optimum R-values for your area, as illustrated on pages 76-77.

Sometimes, however, simply adding insulation to the right R-value is not enough. If you find that your existing insulation has been soaked by moisture or partly melted by fire, it is best to remove it if you can and substitute new material.

You may have even more unpleasant surprises awaiting you when you peer behind walls, ceilings and floors of an old house. Sawdust and rags—both highly flammable—have been used as insulation in the past. So have stacks of bricks, which have almost no insulating value at all. Adobe and sod were the insulation in many Western homes, and solid wood planks and corncobs filled that role in early New England dwellings. All of these materials should be removed, if possible, and replaced with modern insulation.

Measuring inside a Wall

1 **Cutting an opening.** To check the insulation of a finished wall, use the existing openings around electrical outlet boxes. First turn off power to the circuit serving that outlet; if you are not sure of the circuits, turn off the main electric switch at the service panel. Then unscrew the cover plate to expose the metal box. You will usually find a crack between the sides of the box and the plaster or wallboard. Widen this crack to about ¼ of an inch with a cold chisel and a hammer.

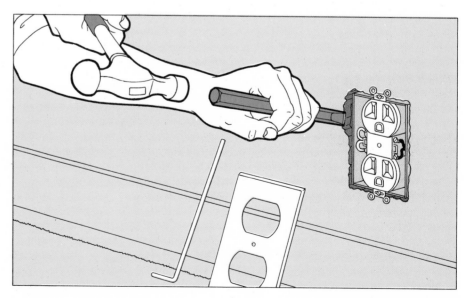

2 **Determining the type of insulation.** Use a flashlight to see if any insulation is visible inside the crack. If you find a vapor barrier (*pages 70-71*) just inside the opening, you probably have blanket or batt-type insulation. The only way to add more insulation is to remove the wall completely or to blow in loose fill through holes in the exterior wall (*pages 86-88*).

If you find insulation without a vapor barrier, you probably have loose fill or foamed-in-place insulation. To identify the type of loose fill, insert a hooked length of stiff wire into the wall cavity and pull out a sample. To find out whether the fill has settled in the wall, leaving uninsulated gaps near the ceiling, place the palm of your hand against the wall every 3 feet, starting at the baseboard and working toward the ceiling; for a more precise test, use a thermometer, with its bare bulb pressed against the wall and the back of the bulb insulated from the heat of the room by two or three layers of tape. If you notice a sharp temperature drop (i.e., 10° or more) toward the ceiling, the fill has settled; the cavity should be refilled.

Measuring under a Floor

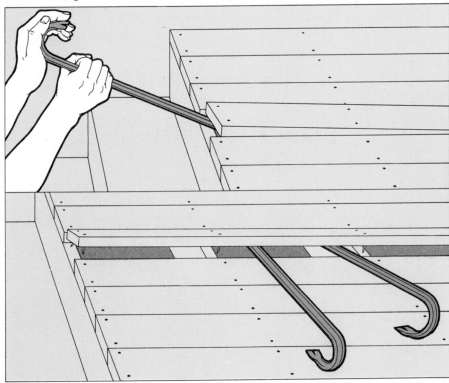

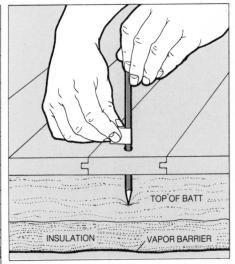

Butted floorboards. If your attic floorboards are simply nailed alongside each other, use a pair of pry bars to free a board without damaging it. At the attic entrance, work one of the bars under the board and pry the end up as far as you can. Move to a new position from which you can insert the second bar underneath the raised side of the board and pry the board upward slowly but

firmly. Repeat the process until you have raised the entire board from the joists below it. The insulation can now be identified and measured with a ruler. Afterward, nail the board back in its original position.

Tongue-and-groove floorboards. Do not attempt to raise a board of tongue-and-groove flooring. Drill a ½-inch hole in the middle of a board between two joists; insert a sharpened pencil into the hole, point first, until you feel resistance as the pencil touches the top level of the insulation. Use masking tape to mark the pencil level with the floor surface. Then push the pencil down through the insulation until the point reaches the vapor barrier. (If the vapor barrier is not flush with the ceiling below, you will feel additional resistance as the point penetrates the barrier.) Mark the pencil again at floor level and withdraw the pencil; the distance between the marks is the thickness of the insulation. Use a hooked length of wire to remove a piece of material for identification. Plug the hole with a dowel.

How Much Insulation Do You Need?

Unfortunately, there is no single formula for determining the precise amount of insulation you need. Variations in climate, in the cost of fuel and in the efficiency of a heating system, all will figure in the decision. Even the type and site of a house can make a difference. A two-story house needs less insulation than a one-story house with the same interior area because its roof is smaller. A house at the bottom of a hill is usually colder in winter than its neighbor near the top, and a house near a body of water tends to be chilled more by onshore winds than one farther inland. Another factor is the amount of heat you need for comfort: one family may be comfortable at 65°, another at 70°—and that 5° difference may justify extra insulation.

Most families settle for the average insulation R-values *(pages 70-71)* over a large geographical zone *(opposite, top)*. Basically, these are climatic zones, but a number of different yardsticks are used to establish them. For fall, winter and spring, when insulation does most of its work, the most important yardstick is the degree day—the number of degrees between the average temperature of a single day and 65°. On a day with an average temperature of 42°, for example, the degree-day reading is 65 minus 42, or 23. When totaled for an entire year, degree days range from less than 2,500 in the southern United States to more than 10,000 in some parts of Canada and Alaska—and the insulation requirement rises with the number of degree days.

A second yardstick for cold weather is the winter design temperature: the lowest temperature that can reasonably be expected during the course of an entire winter, based on the records of past winters. Ranging from 40° in Florida to –50° in parts of Canada and Alaska, these temperatures can also affect requirements in an insulation zone.

With the spread of air conditioning, still other climatic yardsticks have come into use. In some localities summer design temperatures may soar to 100°; annual cooling hours—the total number of hours when the temperature rises to more than 80° and air conditioners are likely to be in operation—may come to 1,500 or more. Like the cold of winter, these extreme temperatures call for insulation—in this case, to keep air-conditioning costs low. For that reason a house in Miami, situated in a warm climate, needs more insulation than a house in San Francisco, in a mild one.

The remaining yardsticks for establishing insulation requirements are financial rather than climatic. Seasonal temperatures are much the same from year to year; insulation and fuel costs are not, and an investment in insulation that seems high today may seem reasonable as the price of energy climbs. Therefore, the recommendations for R-values of ceiling, wall and floor insulation in the chart opposite, below, are based on projected as well as present savings in fuel costs, and assume that energy prices will continue to increase.

Step One: Find Your Zone on the Map

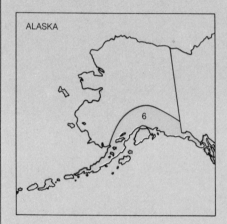

A pattern of six zones. This map indicates six numbered zones, ranging from subtropical Florida, where heating costs are negligible but air-conditioning costs are high, to parts of Canada and Alaska where the ground never thaws. For the insulation suggested for use in each zone, see the chart at right below.

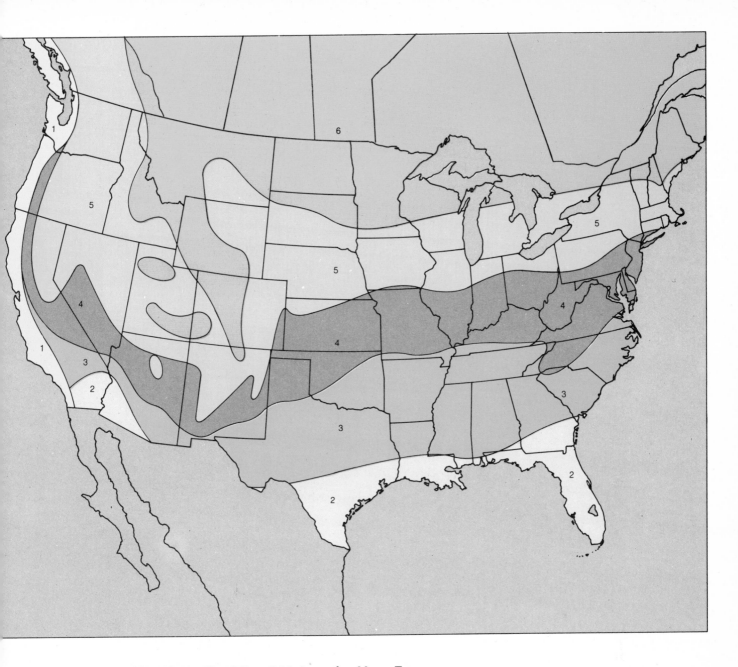

Step Two: Find the R-Values for Your Zone

Zone	A ceiling below a roof or unheated attic	An exterior wall	A floor over an unheated basement or crawl space
1	R-19	R-11	R-11
2	R-26	R-13	R-11
3	R-26	R-19	R-13
4	R-30	R-19	R-19
5	R-33	R-19	R-22
6	R-38	R-19	R-22

How much insulation you should have. Locate the insulation zone of your home on the map above, then use this chart to find R-values recommended for the zone by government and industry specialists. To translate R-values into insulation specifications, see pages 70-71. If you live on the border between two zones, choose the higher rather than the lower values.

The Attic: Where Insulation Pays Off Most

Attic insulation is the most important in the house, not only because heat is lost up through the attic in winter, but also because attics build up heat in summer. So insulating your house begins here, whether your attic is simply an unfinished, unheated, unused space without a floor *(below)*; an unfinished, probably unheated, storage area with a floor *(pages 80-81)*; or a finished room, heated and perhaps even occupied *(pages 84-85)*. And do not forget the stairway or access hatch; in most homes, it acts as a gaping hole for heat transfer. However, do not seal your attic space completely; adequate insulation must be combined with adequate ventilation *(pages 52-58)*.

The most practical insulation for the attic is batts of glass fiber or mineral wool *(page 71)* that come with an attached vapor barrier. Loose fill is often spread into the spaces between floor joists, but it requires the addition of a separate vapor barrier. Batts are more convenient to handle than blankets in the confined spaces under the roof, since they are pre-cut to maneuverable lengths. Batts are also used as an extra layer over existing floor insulation; for this application, slash any vapor barrier to avoid trapping moisture between insulation layers. Remember that the packages of batts appear compact, but they will expand more than four times their thickness once opened; unwrap one package at a time.

If your attic is unfinished and unfloored, you will probably need to install temporary lighting and flooring. Hang one or more safety lights, set walkway boards across several joists (the exposed ceiling will probably break if you step on it) and lay down other boards to support the insulation. You will need a serrated knife or dull handsaw to cut the batts, and a staple gun. Wear gloves, a breathing mask and goggles, and consider a hard hat: you might hit protruding roofing nails under the eaves.

Installing a vapor barrier. If you use loose fill or batts or blankets lacking a vapor barrier, you must also install strips of polyethylene plastic to block moisture. For the joist spaces in an unfinished floor, cut strips a few inches wider than the floor joists. Lay them into the spaces before installing the insulation. Staple them to the sides of the joists without gaps or bulges. Do not lay a continuous sheet up and over or across the joists Patch gaps and tears with masking tape 2 inches wide. Separate vapor barriers can be similarly installed between wall studs or rafters.

Batts for an Unfinished Floor

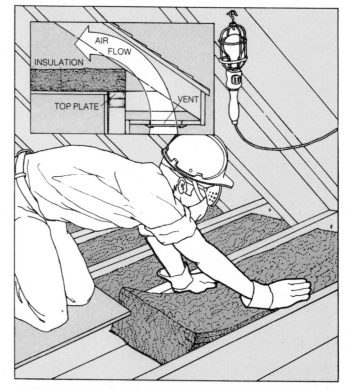

1 **Laying batts between joists.** Start at the eaves on one side of the attic, pushing the batts just far enough in between to cover the top plate *(inset)*. Do not jam the batts tightly against the eaves because that would block the flow of air through the attic space. Install the batts with vapor barrier side down, toward the heated part of the house. Fill several rows at a time while working toward the attic center. Repeat, working in from the opposite eaves. When the batts meet in the center of the attic, compress their ends to butt tightly together.

2 **Cutting batts.** Set the batt on scrap plywood or boards to provide a working surface. Compress the batt as shown below, putting a 2-by-4 or long straightedge tool along the line of the cut. Cut with a sharp serrated knife or dull handsaw.

3 **Fitting batts around obstacles.** Cut the insulation to fit snugly around protruding objects and compress it to slide under wires. Batt ends should butt against each other at cross braces; separate the layers to slide below and above the braces. Wrap a chimney with heavy-duty aluminum foil and add noncombustible insulation.

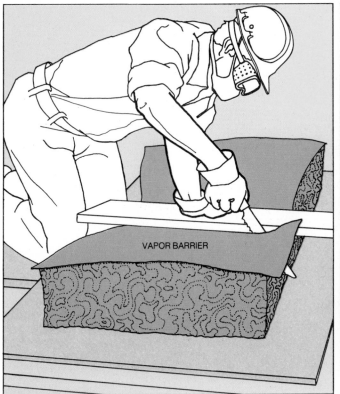

VAPOR BARRIER

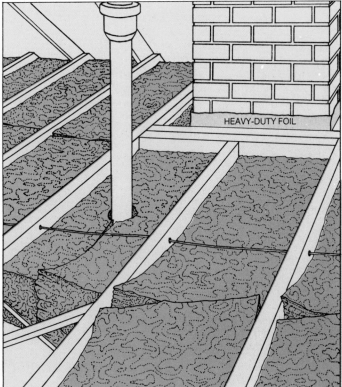

HEAVY-DUTY FOIL

An Extra Layer for Extra Protection

Adding insulation. Top the present layer with loose fill or batts with no vapor barriers; if they have vapor barriers, slash them with a knife so moisture is not trapped within insulation layers. If the existing insulation is level with the tops of the joists, nail 2-by-6 supports to the sides of the joists ever 4 feet along two middle rows. These supports, which should stick up about 6 inches above the joists, will support a new walkway over the new insulation. Lay the new batts at right angles to the joists, following the preceding instructions for laying, cutting and fitting batts.

Insulating an Attic Ceiling

An unfinished attic with a floor can be insulated simply by stapling batts between the studs on the end walls and also between the rafters of the roof *(right)*. But it is more effective to hang insulation below the roof peak, if necessary installing "collar" ceiling beams to support the batts. The space between the beams and the peak of the roof, when combined with the vents that are shown on pages 52-58, will act as a channel to remove excess heat in summer and water vapor in winter. The collar beams can be 2-by-4s nailed across rafters, but if you use 2-by-6s, with ends that are beveled to match the slope of the roof, you will be one step closer to finishing your attic.

Insulating without collar beams. Fit batts between the rafters with the vapor barriers facing you. Do not push the batts all the way to the roof, but leave some air space between the batt and the roof for ventilation. Staple flanges to the edges of the rafters every 6 inches, and butt the ends at the roof peak, overlapping the flanges. Insulate end walls as in Step 3 *(opposite)*.

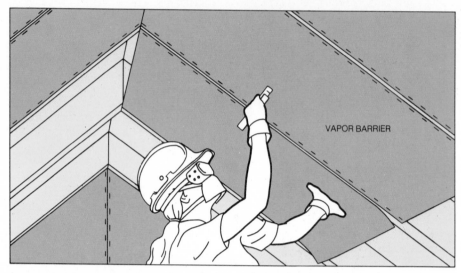

VAPOR BARRIER

Batts for a New Room

1 Installing the beams. Cut 2-by-4s to span each pair of rafters across the attic at a convenient ceiling height, making them long enough to reach the roof sheathing at both ends. Drive nails through the beams into the sides of the rafters.

2 **Installing roof and ceiling batts.** Staple batts of insulation to the edges of the collar beams, with the vapor barriers facing you. Space staples at 6-inch intervals. Then staple batts between rafters from the collar beams down to the floor. Do not try to run continuous batts up the rafters and across the beams; they will gap. Tape the edges of insulation where the collar beams and rafters meet, to make a continuous vapor barrier.

3 **Insulating the end walls.** Install batts between the wall studs with the vapor barrier facing you. Trim the batts to fit all angles, and wedge pieces of batts around windows or louvers.

Insulating an Attic Access

Access to an unfinished attic—whether it is an open stairwell or just a hatchway—can be a major hole in the swathing of insulation that holds heat in or out, undermining the hard work you put in packing batts between floor joists, collar beams and rafters.

If there is a stairway, make sure it has a door, and glue a rigid insulation board to the back. If possible, fill the spaces under and around the treads of the steps with loose fill (right). Hatchways present more of a challenge. The best way to seal cracks around the opening is to build an insulated box in the attic that encloses it as well as any stairs or ladder it contains. The top of the box is provided with a hinged lid you push up as you climb.

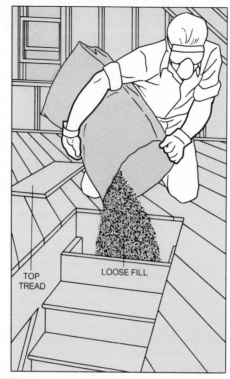

TOP TREAD   LOOSE FILL

Insulating stairs. Pry up the top tread and pour loose fill to fill the cavity under the stairs. Spread the insulation with a long-handled rake as you proceed. If the wall studs on either side of the staircase are exposed and uninsulated, fit batts between them (page 85); if there is a door, glue rigid insulation boards to its back (page 94).

A Box for a Hatchway

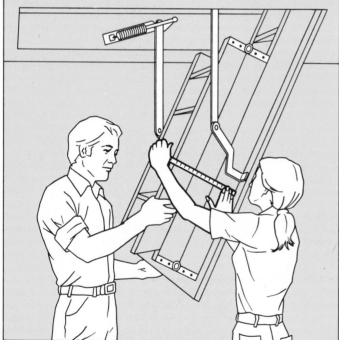

1 Measuring the stairway depth. If the hatchway contains pull-down steps, lower them but do not unfold the folding type. Measure the thickness to determine how much clearance the stairs need when they are raised into the attic.

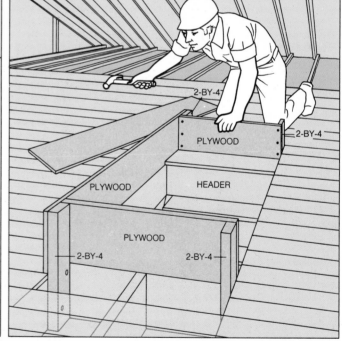

2-BY-4   2-BY-4   PLYWOOD   HEADER   PLYWOOD   PLYWOOD   2-BY-4   2-BY-4

2 Building the box frame. Remove flooring (page 64) and insulation from around the stair opening. Saw four 2-by-4 uprights long enough to rise above the floor joists 2 inches more than the measurement made in Step 1. Nail an upright to each joist behind the corners at the ends of the hatchway. At the top of the stairs, place the uprights 10 inches back from the opening, to provide a step in the attic. Then nail ½-inch plywood to the uprights. Replace any removed flooring.

3 **Finishing the box.** Cut a length of 2-by-4 to match the height of the plywood; nail it through the plywood into the upright at two corners of the box on the side where the lid will be attached. Then nail to each upright another 2-by-4 that projects 8 inches higher, so that the lid can rest against them when it is open.

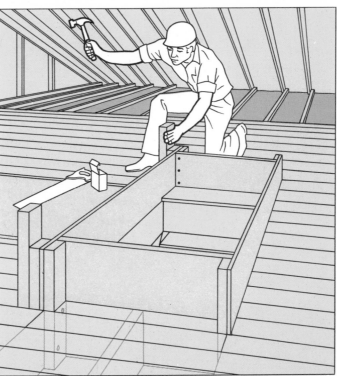

4 **Covering the frame.** Saw a lid from ¼-inch plywood, big enough to extend to the outer edges of the four original uprights. To prevent warping, put a 2-by-4 down one long edge of the lid, nailing through the plywood into the 2-by-4. Attach the other side of the lid with bolt-held hinges to the outside of the frame on the side of the box with the uprights (Step 2). Attach a door handle to the inside of the lid at a point that allows you to conveniently pull the lid down.

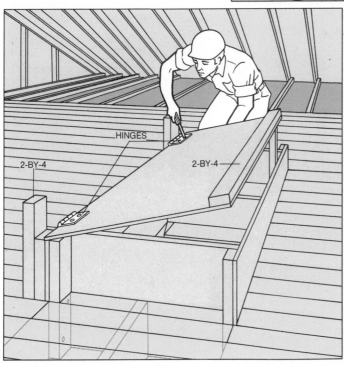

5 **Insulating the box.** Cut two batts slightly longer than the short sides of the box and compress them snugly between the end uprights, with their vapor barriers against the plywood. Trim two more batts to fit the long sides of the box and staple their flanges to the sides. Place another batt or batts, vapor barrier down, on top of the lid and staple the flanges to the lid.

Insulating a Finished Attic

Insulating a finished attic is no more complicated than working in an unfinished one, except for getting to the places you must insulate. You will have to cut out passageways in the ceiling and side—or knee—walls.

Once you have gained access through the knee walls to the outer unfinished attic floor, you insulate as shown on pages 78-79 for unfinished attic floors. Batts also are installed behind knee walls

and on top of the level ceiling. Batts cannot be used for the sloping sections of ceilings because roofing nails are likely to rip them. Instead, throw loose fill into this space from above the flat ceiling. This can only be done after installing the batts behind the knee wall so the tops of the batts will keep the loose fill from falling behind the knee wall. If your attic space is too small to maneuver in, blow in loose fill (pages 86-88).

KNEE WALL

A well-insulated attic room. Batts should be installed in all the outer attic space you can get to: above the flat attic ceiling, behind the low knee walls, and between the joists of the attic floor beyond the knee walls. Then loose fill can be dropped down the hard-to-reach sloped ceiling. Unless you left passageways to the outer attic when you finished the room, cut access panels (*dotted lines*) on the ceiling and knee walls.

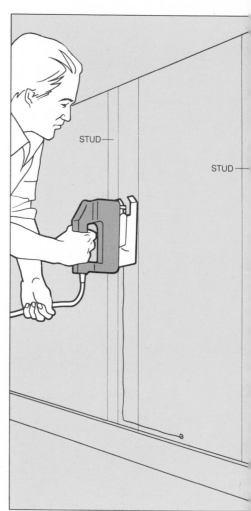

STUD

STUD

1 Cutting an opening. Drill a ⅜-inch hole through the ceiling or at the bottom of the knee wall. If there is a wall switch, do not cut near it. Cut across to the nearest joist or stud, then cut alongside it to the top or bottom. Cut across to the next joist or stud, and complete the rectangle. Remove the section of wallboard and staple a batt to its back, with the vapor barrier where it will face toward the room.

2 Installing batts in walls and outer floor. Fit batts between the joists of the outer attic floor, with the vapor barrier facing down. Fit unfaced friction-fit batts—designed to be installed without stapling flanges—snugly between the studs of the knee walls, and cover the ceiling with batts, vapor barrier down. Be sure that the top of the batt touches the roof. Make a vapor barrier for the unfaced friction-fit insulation by painting the inside of the attic room with a glossy oil-base enamel and then with alkyd paint.

OUTER ATTIC RAFTERS

OUTER ATTIC FLOOR

3 Repairing the access opening. Working from behind the access opening, toenail a 2-by-4 across one end of the opening, half above and half below the cut edge. Then nail 1-by-2 strips of wood down the length of each joist or stud on the inside passageway edge of the access hole. Align the strips with the 2-by-4 to provide a backstop for the panel when it is replaced.

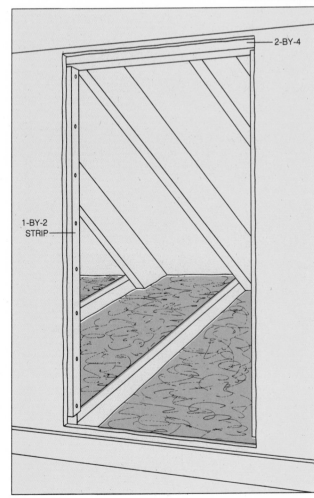

2-BY-4

1-BY-2 STRIP

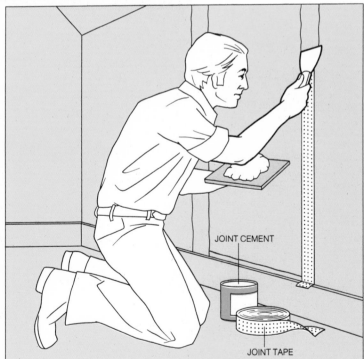

JOINT CEMENT

JOINT TAPE

4 Installing a replacement panel. Working from the finished attic side, set the panel in the wallboard opening against the three strips of wood and nail in place. Cover the joint with perforated joint tape and spread a thin coat of joint cement over the tape with a taping knife as shown above. When the joint cement dries, put on a second layer. Sand the dry cement with fine sandpaper.

Getting Insulation into Finished Walls

While the attic needs insulation more than any other part of the house, exterior walls are next in importance—for comfort and for economy in energy use in most climates. The best time to insulate these walls is during construction, when batts are easily installed between structural members, but the job can be done later. The kind of insulation you use and where you install it depends on how your wall is constructed and whether you prefer to work on the inside or outside of the house.

The walls of a frame house are insulated from the inside, for example, by removing wallboard or other paneling and installing batts of insulation between the studs, but it is generally easier to open part of the wall and stuff it with loose fill. This method works, of course, only on houses constructed in the standard way, with a wood frame and studs that leave air spaces between exterior and interior wall surfaces. If the wall is masonry, put up panels of polystyrene insulation as shown on pages 93 and 94.

Even a cavity wall contains obstructions—fire stops of horizontal pieces to block the spread of flames, as well as plumbing pipes, heating ducts and electrical wires. In many cases, it may be necessary to cut into the wall at several places to fill it completely.

Walls with brick or metal siding outside are best filled by drilling from inside, since the damage done by drilling outside would be difficult to repair. If you have a wood clapboard or shingle siding, however, cut holes from the outside, force in insulation, then replace the removed sections.

Loose fill of rock wool or chopped cellulose is ordinarily used, blown into the cavities with a special machine that can be rented from a building-supply firm or insulation contractors. The cavities also can be filled with plastic foam, but this method requires a professional, since mixing the foam and selecting the right installation pressures are critical operations. Even if you do not apply the insulation, you still may save money by drilling the holes yourself; ask the contractor. Some foam compounds may be fire hazards and should be installed according to local building codes.

If you live in an older frame house, there may be spaces between the studs from the attic down to the basement. Simply close the holes in the basement and drop loose insulation down from the attic to fill the cavities.

If you use loose-fill insulation, make sure there is a vapor barrier between it and the interior of the house to prevent inside moisture from condensing in the insulation and ruining it *(page 71)*. Foam insulation makes its own vapor barrier. The easiest way to provide a vapor barrier is to coat the inside walls first with glossy oil-base enamel, which will seal the wall, then with alkyd paint. At the same time, all cracks around windows, doorframes, baseboards and electrical outlets must be caulked *(pages 18-19)*.

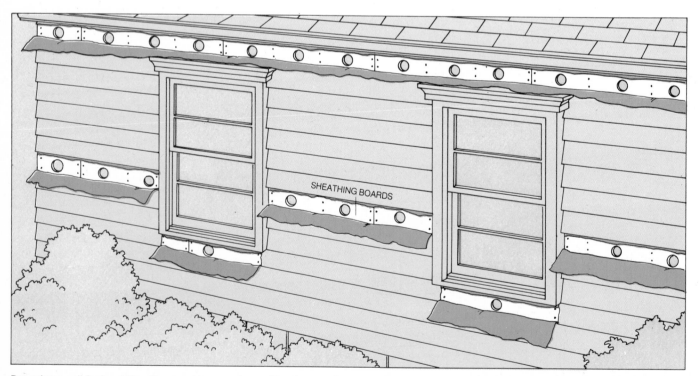

SHEATHING BOARDS

Preparing a wall for insulation. Remove strips of clapboards or shingles at several points on the house, then cut holes through the sheathing boards into the wall cavity *(opposite)*. Begin by taking off the top row of siding all around the house. For a two-story house you must also remove a strip of siding near the ceiling of the first floor. You can identify this strip by drilling a hole with an extension bit all the way through the wall from the inside. Patch the holes later. You also must remove siding below windows and below obstructions within the wall such as fire stops—lengths of 2-by-4s that are nailed horizontally between studs. Such obstructions can be located with the test described overleaf.

Removing shingles. To dislodge a wood shingle, follow the instructions on page 44 for removing a wood roofing shingle. To remove asbestos shingles, which have exposed nails, cut off nailheads with diagonal cutting pliers, and lift the shingles away from the wall to free them from the remaining nail stubs, then slip them down and off the wall. Pull the nail stubs out of the wall with pliers. Remove a row of shingles, then with a utility knife make one horizontal cut in the building paper at the top of the opening and fold it down to expose the sheathing underneath.

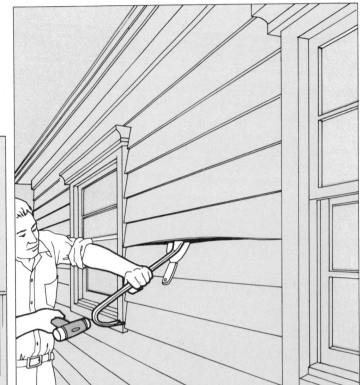

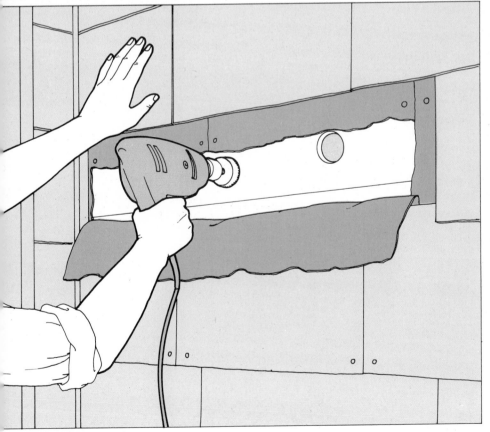

Removing a clapboard. With a mallet, gently tap a wide-blade putty knife into the joint below the clapboard you wish to remove. The clapboards will clamp the putty knife in place while you tap a pry bar into the same joint over the putty knife, which protects the wood beneath. Gently pry up the clapboard ¼ to ½ inch, then remove the pry bar and knife and tap the clapboard back against the wall. This will reveal the location of a clapboard nail. If you have pried directly under a nail, you can pull the nail with the pry bar. If not, repeat the process below the nail and every 16 inches along the wall until you have removed all the nails in a section of clapboard.

Use the putty knife to break the skin of paint along the upper and lower clapboard joints, then pull downward on the clapboard to remove it.

Cutting the holes. Make holes through the sheathing midway between each pair of studs —the location of the nails in the sheathing reveals where the studs are. Cut each hole large enough to admit the nozzle of your blowing equipment —2 or 3 inches in diameter—using a hole saw or a circle cutter (*page 67*) in an electric drill.

Plumbing the cavities. Before blowing in the insulation (*right*), drop a plumb bob on a line through each hole to check for braces, fire stops or other obstructions. Drill another hole below each obstruction so the entire cavity from roof to bottom plate can be filled with insulation.

Blowing in insulation. Insert the nozzle and hose from the blower through the hole and down into the cavity. Gradually fill the cavity with insulation from the bottom up, slowly pulling out the hose as you progress. Tip the nozzle up before withdrawing it, to fill space above the hole.

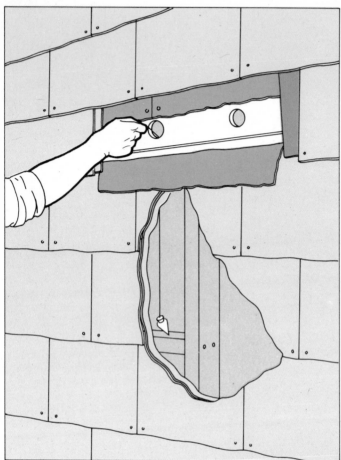

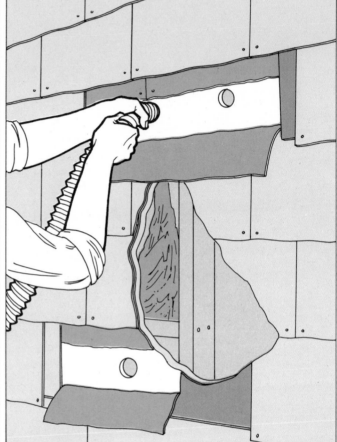

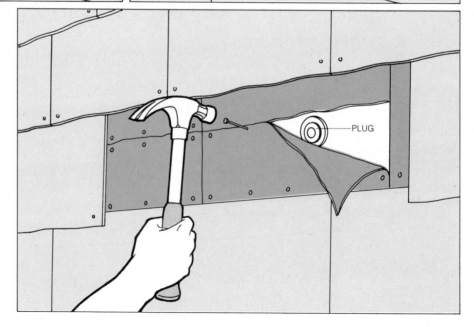

PLUG

Restoring the wall. Close each hole in the sheathing with a tight-fitting plug. Plastic plugs that snap into place, available in stores that sell insulation to contractors, are the most convenient device to use. Staple the building paper back in place and reposition the siding, making sure that the bottom edges line up. If the siding is asbestos shingle or wood clapboards fasten with galvanized nails hammered through the original holes. Nail wood shingles through the bottoms of the shingles in the course above.

Some Pros and Cons of Insulated Siding

Frequently a homeowner is sold the idea that re-siding his house will lower his fuel bills. This may be true—but only if the job is done with insulating backing. Even so, re-siding is not a substitute for a complete insulation system, since it adds only a limited amount of insulation.

If frequent peeling of paint is your reason for re-siding, first correct the moisture problem within the walls *(page 52)*. Otherwise, moisture will increase and cause rotting of the old siding and the house framing.

There are two basic types of siding with insulation: one is a fiberboard backer in panels that are slipped into the air space in the hollow behind each strip of siding as the siding is installed *(bottom)*. This type of insulation is used with metal and vinyl siding. The other kind of insulation is polystyrene laminated to the back of the siding; it comes with aluminum or steel siding only. Generally, the second type has a higher R value *(page 70)*, and the polystyrene has the additional advantage of not retaining moisture as the fiberboard may. The insulating qualities of fiberboard backer and laminated polystyrene turned out to be an incidental benefit—they were developed to strengthen the siding and reduce the noise of expansion and contraction.

Some additional insulation is provided if new siding is attached over 1-by-3 furring strips nailed through the old siding to the studs inside the walls *(top)*. The furring strips create an air space of about ¾ inch. Such furring strips must be provided for siding applied over existing asbestos shingles or stucco—they make an essential nailing surface for the new siding—and they are sometimes used on other types of walls.

Some siding contractors recommend first laying a thin sheet of perforated aluminum foil over the old siding—but it must be perforated, otherwise it acts as a vapor barrier on the wrong side of the wall, trapping moisture within the walls where it is not wanted. Like any additional layer of skin that you wrap around a house, it adds insulation, but again only a minimal amount unless the siding is put on airtight.

Down Below: Barriers to Stop Cold, Conserve Fuel

Because warm air rises, some homeowners assume that a well-insulated attic is all they need. But an uninsulated basement or crawl space is an expensive nuisance. If it is heated, it needs insulation as much as any outside room. If it is both unheated and uninsulated, it may make the floors above it cold, wasting fuel and causing chills.

The worst offenders are spaces with dirt floors. Cover such floors with plastic sheeting—preferably 6-mil opaque polyethylene. Then, if the space is unheated, install vents in the walls (page 59) to prevent condensation on basement beams and ground-floor walls. Finally, apply the insulation itself.

In a heated basement or crawl space, lay the insulation against the walls (pages 93-95). In an unheated space, it goes against the ceiling (below), in batts or blankets pushed, vapor-barrier side up, between the floor joists overhead and held in place with wire braces.

This ceiling insulation does not meet all the problems of an unheated space. All heating and air-conditioning ducts should also be insulated. You may be able to buy duct blankets 2 inches thick for this purpose. If you cannot get them, cut your own from the same insulation you used between the floor joists, cutting sections to fit around the ducts, not along them. For minimum waste in cutting, use blankets rather than batts. Make sure the vapor barrier faces you, that all exposed duct surfaces are covered and that seams are sealed with duct tape. If ducts hang so low that they might be bumped into, wrap them with 15-pound building paper to protect the vapor barrier against punctures.

In cold climates, water pipes in an unheated basement or crawl space may also need insulation to prevent supply lines from freezing and to conserve heat in hot-water lines. Use rigid cylindrical felt sleeves, sold in 3-foot lengths and in a wide range of diameters. The sleeves come with an outer canvas jacket that overlaps to help form a heat seal, but to protect them against moisture you should add a second jacket made from ordinary aluminum foil.

Insulating the Unheated Spaces

Working with batts and braces. Push a batt of insulation, vapor-barrier side up, into the spaces between the floor joists overhead. The barrier should just touch the subflooring. Every 16 inches or so install wire braces—cut from wire clothes hangers a bit longer than joist spacing—so that they barely touch the blankets; crushing insulation reduces its effectiveness.

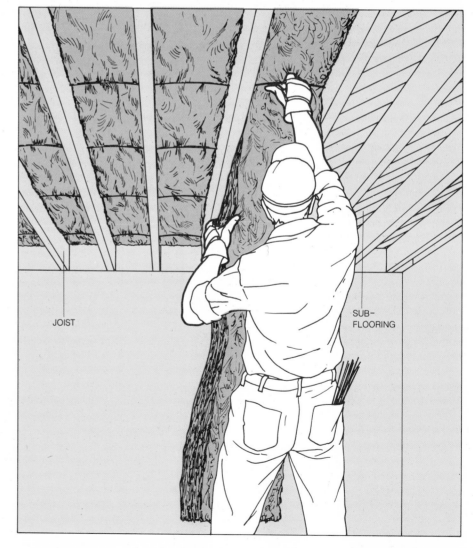

JOIST

SUB-
FLOORING

Wraps for Ducts

1 Working with blankets and tape. To cover a duct, use sections of insulation cut from long blankets and wrapped crosswise around the duct. To find the length of each section, multiply the thickness of the insulation by four and add the circumference of the duct. To find the number of sections you need, divide the length of the duct by the width of the blanket. Wrap the sections around the duct, vapor barrier out, and seal the seams between the sections with duct tape.

2 Cutting the section for the duct end. Before finishing the horizontal duct, lay a patch of insulation against the furnace side of the vertical duct that rises into the floor overhead. Cut a final section of insulation to fit around the bottom and sides of the horizontal duct end and extend beyond the end to a distance half the width of the duct. Tape this section in place and cut the insulation beyond the end of the duct along the dotted lines shown in the drawing below.

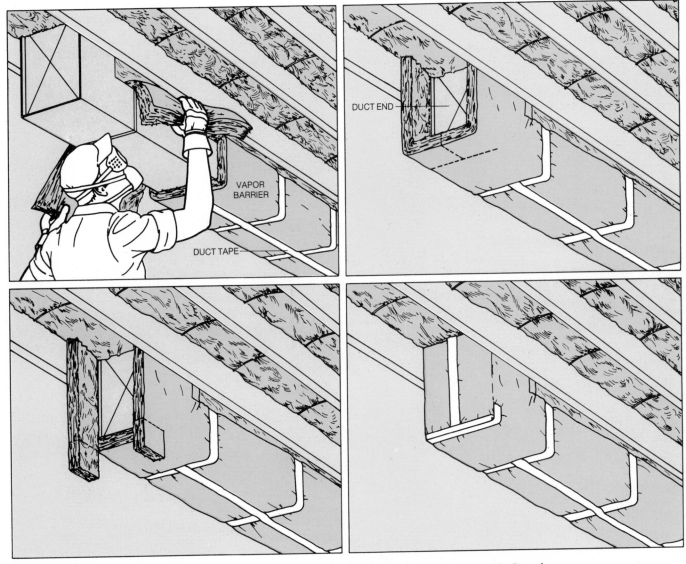

3 Trimming the tabs. Cut off the excess insulation at the end of the duct—two tabs hanging down from the bottom of the wrapped portion —as indicated by the dotted lines (*above*).

4 Sealing the end of the duct. Fold the flaps of insulation beyond the end of the duct to cover the front of the vertical duct. If the final section does not fit the duct, so that the flaps do not meet, cut a piece of insulation to fill the gap. If the flaps are too wide, trim them to meet. Seal the last seams with duct tape and, if the insulated ducts hang below the top of your head, cover them with 15-pound building paper.

Insulating a recessed duct. To insulate a duct nestled between two joists, cut blanket sections long enough to reach the outside edges of the adjoining joists. Push the insulation an inch or so back from the ends of each section, leaving the vapor barrier intact. Wrap the insulation around the bottom of the duct with the vapor barrier out, and staple the exposed barrier to the bottoms of the joists. For the part that enters the floor overhead, cut a section that extends beyond the edge of the duct for a distance equal to the thickness of the insulation; cover the end of the duct with a patch of insulation and seal all seams with duct tape.

Sleeves for Piping

1 A close-fitting sleeve. Clean the pipes, scraping off any rust and sealing all leaks, however small. Cover the pipes with lengths of cylindrical pipe insulation and glue the lap down tightly. To make short sections of insulation, cut the insulation with a utility knife or a handsaw.

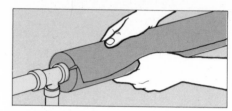

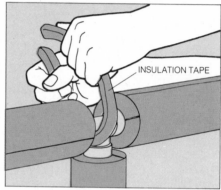

INSULATION TAPE

2 Taping the fittings. Cover the pipe fittings with insulation tape ¼ inch thick. Be sure to cover the fittings completely: no part should be exposed to air. To complete the job, wrap both the pipe and the fittings in aluminum foil.

A Vapor Barrier for a Dirt Floor

Laying plastic strips. Cover an unpaved basement or crawl-space floor with strips of 6-mil polyethylene plastic, with overlaps of about 6 inches. Strips about 3 feet wide are easiest to work with. Use duct tape to fasten the end of each strip to the wall 2 inches above the ground, and tape the plastic down where the wall meets the ground. Trim off excess plastic and weight the overlaps with bricks or stones.

Floors in older houses and in houses where air conditioning is used frequently have some moisture content; in these cases, cover only about 70 per cent of the soil area in order to avoid a sharp drop in the moisture content, which would cause the floors to shrink or warp.

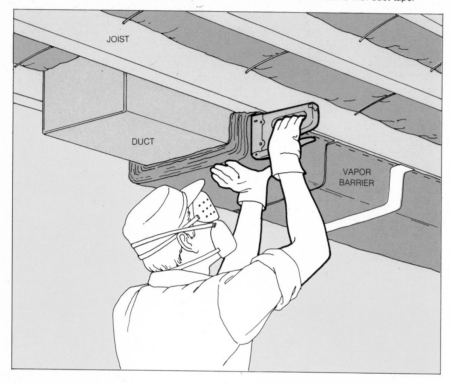

JOIST

DUCT

VAPOR BARRIER

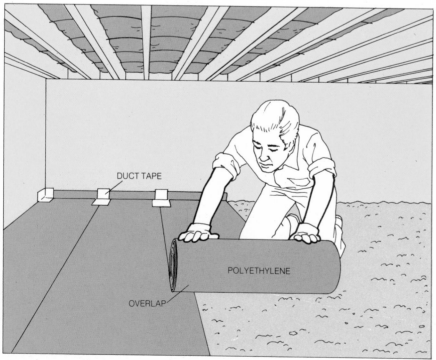

DUCT TAPE

POLYETHYLENE

OVERLAP

Insulating the Warm Spaces

Since their functions are dissimilar, heated basements and heated crawl spaces are not insulated alike. A heated unfinished basement, potentially part of the living area of a house, must be insulated with compact materials in a way that makes finishing the space easy. A heated crawl space in a one-story house can never be lived in, of course, but it can be part of the house heating system. In some houses it serves as a huge duct, called a plenum, through which heat passes on its way to the living area above. Even a well-insulated plenum is relatively inefficient. Before insulating a heated crawl space, consider the advantages of ducts to carry the heat from its source to the living area—the ductwork may save enough fuel to compensate for its cost. If ducts cannot be installed, you can greatly reduce heat loss by covering the ground with a polyethylene vapor barrier, and by draping the walls and part of the ground with insulation blankets as shown on page 95.

For insulating the walls of a heated basement, the material commonly used is rigid foamed plastic. It is installed between furring strips, to which gypsum wallboard (not wood paneling) is nailed, covering and protecting the flammable plastic from fire. Be sure to get board with a Class A fire-rating stamp; it has the lowest rate of combustion. The space between the top of the wall and the subflooring is filled with flanged blankets.

Heated Basements

1 **Attaching furring strips.** Cut 2-by-¾-inch furring strips to frame each window and load a caulking gun with construction adhesive. Then run a bead of adhesive around the window and press furring strips into the adhesive. In the same way, apply furring strips in all corners and at the tops and bottoms of walls. Within this framing, mount additional furring strips in a grid pattern to fit the panels of rigid insulation board—usually 2 by 4 feet. If necessary, use a carpenter's level and a plumb bob to check the horizontal and vertical alignment of the strips.

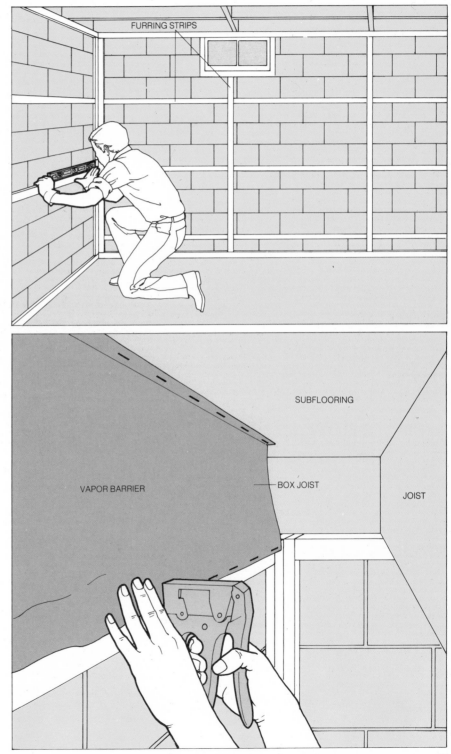

FURRING STRIPS

SUBFLOORING

VAPOR BARRIER

BOX JOIST

JOIST

2 **Insulating the box joists.** On walls that run in the same direction as the joists, the spaces between the top of the wall and the subflooring are called box joists. Use one-piece strips of flanged blanket for insulation. Install the blankets with the vapor barrier facing you and the insulation tucked into the contours of the space. At 6-inch intervals, staple one flange to the subflooring, the other to the top of the furring strip frame.

3 Insulating headers. The spaces enclosed by the ends of joists, the top of the wall and the sub-flooring, called headers, are insulated with sections of insulation blankets cut with a 1-inch overlap over the top of the furring-strip frame. Fit the sections between joists and staple the existing flanges to the joist sides. At the bottom of each section, push the fluffy insulation back an inch or so to form a bottom flange and then staple this flange to the furring frame.

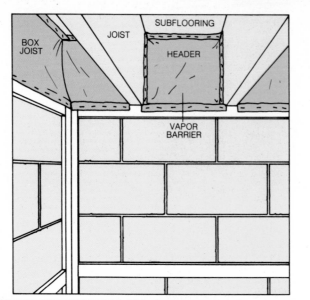

4 Fitting the rigid insulation. Apply construction adhesive to the backs of the insulation boards in the amount and pattern specified by the manufacturer—a common pattern is shown below. Mount the insulation on the wall between the furring strips, cutting the boards to size with a utility knife or a handsaw. The boards must fill the spaces between strips snugly.

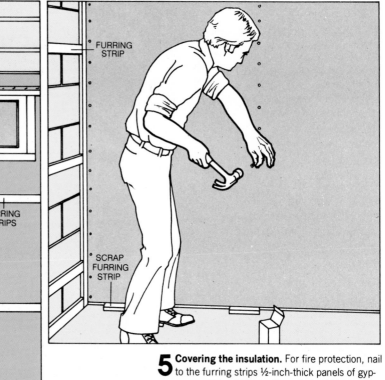

5 Covering the insulation. For fire protection, nail to the furring strips ½-inch-thick panels of gypsum wallboard. The wallboard should be used even if you plan to cover it with modern paneling. When attaching the wallboard, support the bottom edges temporarily on scraps of furring strip. When you pull the scraps from under the panels, the ¾-inch space left will protect the wall from any moisture that accumulates on the floor.

94

Heated Crawl Spaces

1 Insulating the box-joist walls. Lay single strips of polyethylene vapor barrier *(page 92)* along the ground next to the box-joist walls—the walls that run parallel to the joists. Then insulate these walls with sections of insulation blankets cut to the height of the crawl space from the ground to the subfloor. Fasten the sections to the walls, with vapor-barrier side facing you, by setting narrow strips of scrap wood along the top of each section, and nailing through the wood and the insulation to the box joist.

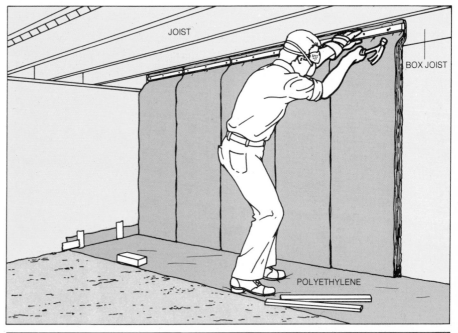

2 Insulating the corners. Starting at the end of the crawl space farthest from the exit, install corner blankets with one side butting against the box-joist insulation and the top flush to the subflooring. Trim the blankets to fit around the joists and fill in the corners with scrap insulation. Run these blankets down the walls and along the plastic strip to meet in the middle of the room. At the meeting point and at the bases of the walls, weight both strips of insulation down with bricks.

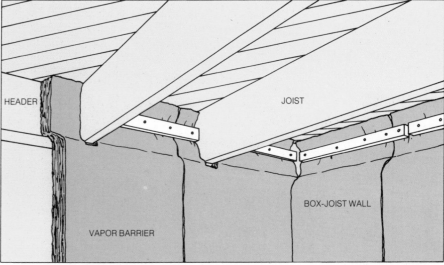

3 Completing the header walls. Lay a second strip of polyethylene vapor barrier on the ground and install a second width of insulation blankets to the header walls; in these and succeeding widths, run the insulation only 2 feet onto the floor. Continue laying polyethylene and installing insulation toward the exit until you reach the opposite box-joist wall; there, install two blankets *(Step 2)* extending across the polyethylene to meet midway.

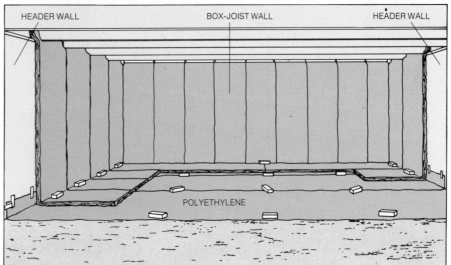

Energy-Saving Window Covers

The windows in most homes are year-round energy wasters. During the cold months, 25 to 30 per cent of a typical house's heat seeps out through the windows; when it is hot outdoors, unwanted warmth in the form of sunlight follows the same route indoors.

One of the simplest and most effective ways to block heat passage through windows is to cover the glass completely with an opaque insulating material. Shades made from lightweight fabric insulation or shutters made from rigid foam drastically reduce heat loss—and heating bills—on cold nights. In rooms where you are willing to sacrifice the view, these window coverings will obstruct incoming sunlight on very hot days, cutting air-conditioning bills significantly.

Coupled with the extra layers of glazing provided by interior or exterior storm windows (pages 98-104), opaque insulators can increase a window's R-value (page 70) to a level close to that of the surrounding walls.

A variety of window shades can be fashioned from fabric insulation; the accordion-pleated Roman shade (right) is an example. You can buy custom-made shades from solar-energy-equipment dealers or—if you possess simple sewing skills—make them yourself.

The fabric insulation—made of two layers of polyester fiber that sandwich a plastic-film vapor barrier—is sold in large sheets at fabric and shade stores. Cover the insulation on the room side with drapery fabric. The rest of the hardware—nylon shade cord and rings, eye screws, adhesive-backed magnetic strips—is available at most hardware stores.

Two types of indoor shutters offer an alternative to fabric shades. Pop-in panels and hinged bifold shutters can be made from inexpensive styrene foam board, the stuff of the common picnic cooler. Slightly more expensive, but more effective, are urethane foam or foil-sided polyisocyanurate foam, sold by solar-energy-equipment dealers under such trade names as Thermax and R Max.

Pop-in panels consisting of a single section of uncovered insulation (page 97, top) are the simplest shutters to make, but they have several disadvantages. To remove them during the day, you must take them down and store them. They also tend to shrink and warp after long periods of use. Bifold shutters made of rigid foam covered with plywood veneer take longer to build, but they are sturdier, more attractive and can be opened to let in light without being dismantled.

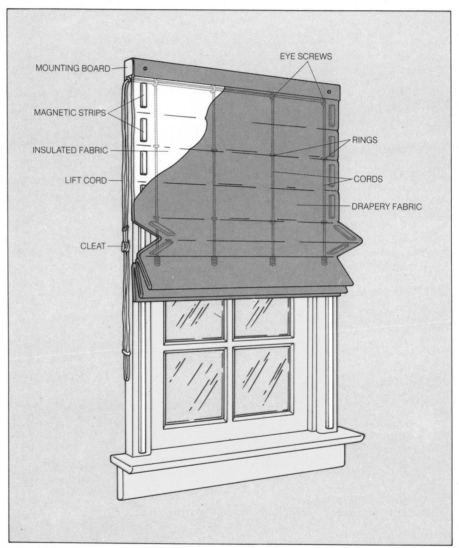

A Roman shade with a magnetic seal. A pleated shade, its inside surface covered with drapery fabric, hangs from a 1-by-2 mounting board screwed to the wall above the window frame. The shade is raised and lowered by four nylon cords threaded through vertical rows of ½-inch rings sewed to the back of the shade; the cords are threaded through a row of eye screws on the bottom edge of the mounting board and then knotted together at one side of the shade to make a lift cord. Lifted, the shade folds into pleats; to keep the shade raised, the lift cord is wound around a cleat secured to the window frame or to the wall. When the shade is lowered, magnetic strips sewed into the shade's side seams and mounted on the window frame keep the shade edges pressed tight against the casing to seal the window against leaks. A metal bar sewed into the hem holds the shade snug against the sill.

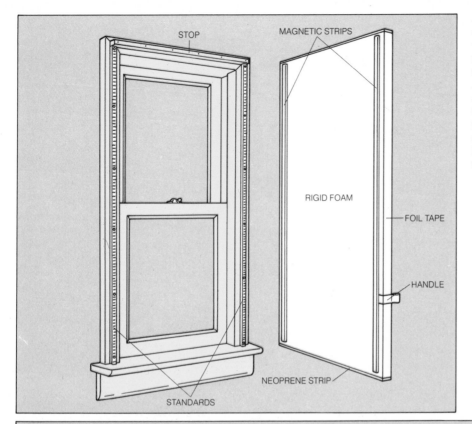

STOP

MAGNETIC STRIPS

RIGID FOAM

FOIL TAPE

HANDLE

NEOPRENE STRIP

STANDARDS

A pop-in panel of rigid foam. Cut to fit flat against the window frame, a panel of ¾-inch rigid foam is held in place by magnetic tape strips mounted on the outside face of the panel and metal shelf standards screwed to the casing. Aluminum-foil tape covers the panel's vertical edges; adhesive-backed neoprene strips form leakproof seals where the bottom edge of the panel meets the sill and where the top edge meets a stop screwed to the upper casing. A loop of duct tape makes a handle for removing the panel from the window.

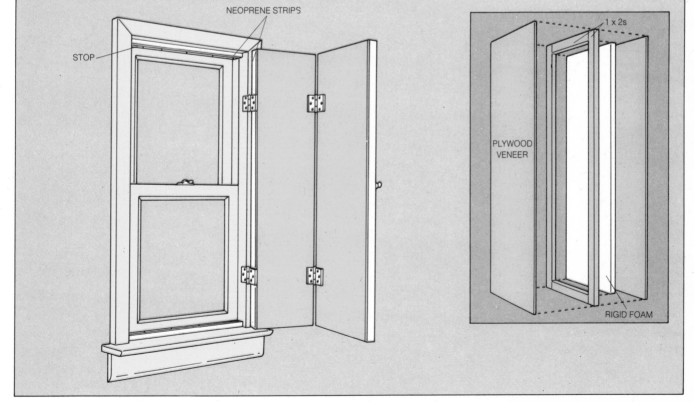

NEOPRENE STRIPS

STOP

1 x 2s

PLYWOOD VENEER

RIGID FOAM

A bifold shutter of foam and veneer. Two hinged shutter panels cut to fit against the inside edges of the casing fold away from the window to admit sunlight, and close against weather-stripped stops to seal the window tightly. Each shutter panel is made from a section of ¾-inch rigid foam edged by a frame of kiln-dried 1-by-2s and faced on both sides by ⅛-inch plywood veneer (*inset*). Neoprene weather stripping covers the vertical edges of the panels. A knob screwed to the inside face of the unhinged panel makes the shutter easy to pull open.

Double-Duty Insulators: Storm Windows and Doors

A second layer of glass over the windows and doors of a house reduces by as much as 50 per cent the amount of heat that passes through these openings, saving on energy needed to heat the house in winter—and to cool it in summer.

You can save money by making your own storm windows (pages 100-103), but there is little advantage to building your own storm doors; homemade ones are difficult to frame and hang. It makes more sense to buy ready-made doors at a building-supply store and install them in the doorframes of your house (page 105).

Storm windows can be constructed with frames of wood, aluminum or plastic to fit either outside or inside the house, and can be glazed with glass or plastic. Wood frames—of exterior-grade plywood—take more time to make, but wood is a better insulator than aluminum, the framing commonly used, and matches more closely the wood window casings of most houses.

Aluminum frames, on the other hand, are not only easier to make but require less maintenance than wood ones. Aluminum storm-window sash is available at hardware stores in 6-, 8- and 10-foot lengths. The frames are built much like picture frames, but they are easier to assemble because special fasteners, called corner locks, hold the pieces together. Plastic frames are generally used only if the storm sash is to be installed inside.

For storm windowpanes, use double-strength glass or transparent plastic ¼ inch thick. Glass, available in sizes-listed in the chart opposite, is less expensive than plastic and less likely to scratch. Plastic, however, will not shatter (and is required indoors by building codes in some localities). Both glass and plastic are cut to size using similar techniques, but you need a glass-cutting tool for glass (below).

Storm windows and doors normally require little maintenance aside from occasional washing. Wood frames need a coat of paint every few years, and after several seasons their joints may require reinforcing with metal straps. You can paint aluminum doors and windows, or brush them lightly with steel wool every year to remove any signs of oxidation and coat them with a protective layer of paste wax. If you store your storm windows during the summer, number them and the windows they match so you can pair them easily next season for a perfect fit.

The Delicate Art of Cutting Glass

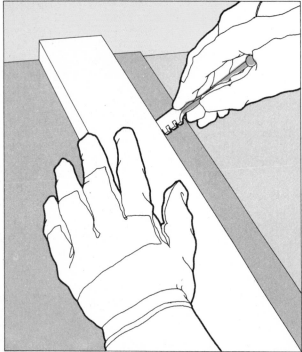

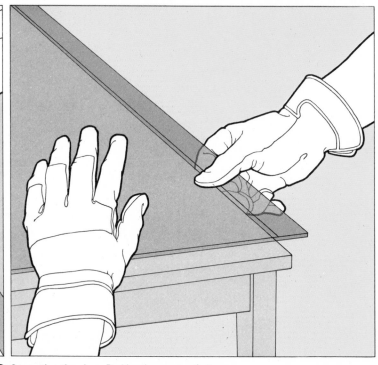

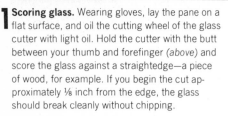

1 Scoring glass. Wearing gloves, lay the pane on a flat surface, and oil the cutting wheel of the glass cutter with light oil. Hold the cutter with the butt between your thumb and forefinger (above) and score the glass against a straightedge—a piece of wood, for example. If you begin the cut approximately ⅛ inch from the edge, the glass should break cleanly without chipping.

2 Separating the glass. Position the pane so that the score line lies along the edge of your work surface. Hold the glass against the surface with one hand and gently push on the waste piece with the other to snap the glass along the score.

Glass Sizes

All dimensions in inches

	24	26	28	30	32	34	36	38	40	42	44	46	48
12													
14			●	●	●	●							
16	●						●			●	●	●	●
18	●							●					
20	●						●		●				●
22							●						●
24	●	●	●			●	●					●	●
26	●		●		●					●			
28	●	●		●	●		●		●			●	
30		●	●	●			●			●			
32		●	●	●			●	●	●				●
34	●		●				●					●	
36	●			●	●	●	●			●	●	●	
38			●	●									
40	●				●				●	●			●
42		●	●	●						●	●		
44							●			●			
46	●			●		●	●						●
48	●			●			●	●	●			●	
50		●									●		
52							●			●			●
54	●								●				●
56													
58								●					
60							●						
62													
64													
66													●
68													
70													
72							●						

Picking a pane. The table above indicates by dots the sizes of precut, double-strength glass that are often used for storm windows. One dimension (in inches) is given across the top of the table and the other down the side. Thus, you can buy a standard pane 32-by-36 inches, but not 32-by-35 or 32-by-37. If possible, adjust the size of your frames to accommodate these sizes; you will save money wasted on oversized pieces of glass as well as time spent trimming them.

Two Types of Windows

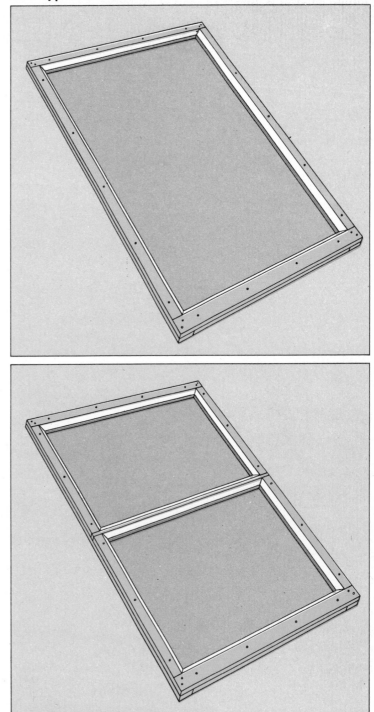

One pane or two. When building wood storm-window frames, you have a choice of designing them for one piece of glass or two. One pane is suitable for small windows, but for windows of average size, or larger, two panes are preferred. The crosspiece makes the frame more rigid and reduces the replacement cost of broken windows. Aluminum frames of the kind shown on pages 102-103 cannot be made with a crosspiece and are limited to a maximum height of 60 inches.

Making Wood Frames

1 Laying out the frame back. Cut two pieces of ½-inch plywood 1½ inches wide and the height of the window to be protected. Cut two pieces of ½-inch plywood 3 inches shorter than the width of the window. One of these pieces should be 1½ inches wide, the other wide enough to reach from the sill to the bottom of the windowpane.

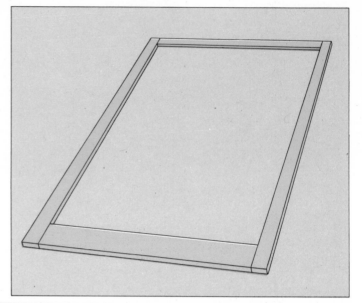

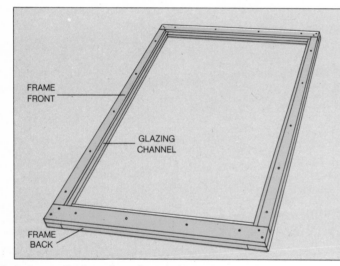

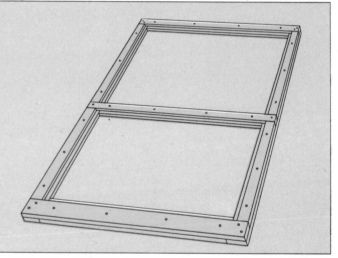

2 Laying out the frame front. For a single-pane window, cut two pieces of ⅝-inch plywood 1 inch wide and 2 inches shorter than the length of the window. Cut two more pieces of ⅝-inch plywood the width of the window, one of them 1 inch wide and the other ½ inch narrower than the bottom piece cut in Step 1. Lay these pieces on top of the frame back so that they overlap the joints in the pieces beneath. The differences in width will leave a ½-inch step, or glazing channel, around the inside of the assembled frame.

For a two-pane window (right, center), cut the long pieces ½ inch shorter than specified above, then cut them in half before fastening them to the back. Cut a piece of ½-inch plywood 1½ inches wide and the same length as the top and bottom pieces of the back. Then cut a piece of ⅝-inch plywood ½ inch wide the full width of the frame. Fasten these pieces together and across the center of the frame with glue and screws (right), leaving a ½-inch glazing channel on both sides of the crosspiece.

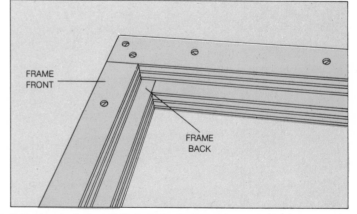

3 Fastening the frames. Drill pilot holes for ¾-inch No. 8 flathead wood screws, two in each corner and one every 8 inches or so around the frame perimeter and along the crosspiece. Bevel the holes with a countersink so the screwheads can be spackled over and painted. Glue the pieces of the frame front to the back, then insert the screws.

4 **Fitting the frame.** Hold the new wood frame against the window casing. Have a helper mark the inside of the storm-window frame wherever the frame overlaps the casing. With a plane or rasp, trim the frame to fit into the window casing along the pencil marks described above. The frame should just clear the window casing on all sides; check the fit frequently while trimming.

5 **Glazing.** Line the glazing channel with a ¼-inch layer of glazing compound, smoothing the putty with a putty knife. Then press the edge of the glass or plastic into the putty.

GLAZING
COMPOUND

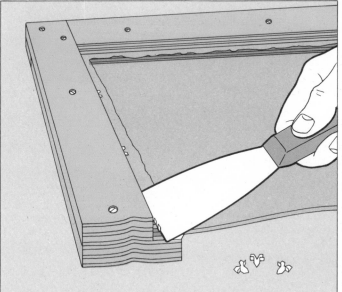

6 **Setting the glazing points.** Lay the triangular metal fasteners called glazing points every 4 inches around the edge of the glass, then push each point into the frame. The push-type points shown can be set with a putty knife; other types require a special tool, usually supplied with the points.

7 **Sealing the pane.** Lay enough glazing compound on the pane to fill the glazing channel. With a putty knife, bevel the compound neatly between the face of the frame and the windowpane, collecting the excess compound in your hand.

Making Aluminum Frames

1 **Cutting the framing.** Remove the rubber gasket, or spline, that comes inside the glazing channel. Mark the width of the window on the framing piece. Using a hacksaw with a fine-tooth blade and a miter box, cut the piece with 45° mitered ends. Cut a second piece of sash the width of the window and two additional lengths the height of the window, mitering them also. File away any burrs that are left by the saw.

2 **Assembling the frame.** With a mallet, hammer a corner lock into one end of a side piece. Insert a 16-penny nail into the glazing channel, using a spare piece of framing to position the nail one thickness from the corner lock.

Tap the nail sharply with a hammer to crimp the sash to the lock (*below*), then attach the bottom of the frame to the other end of the corner lock. Use another corner lock to fasten the top, making three sides of the frame.

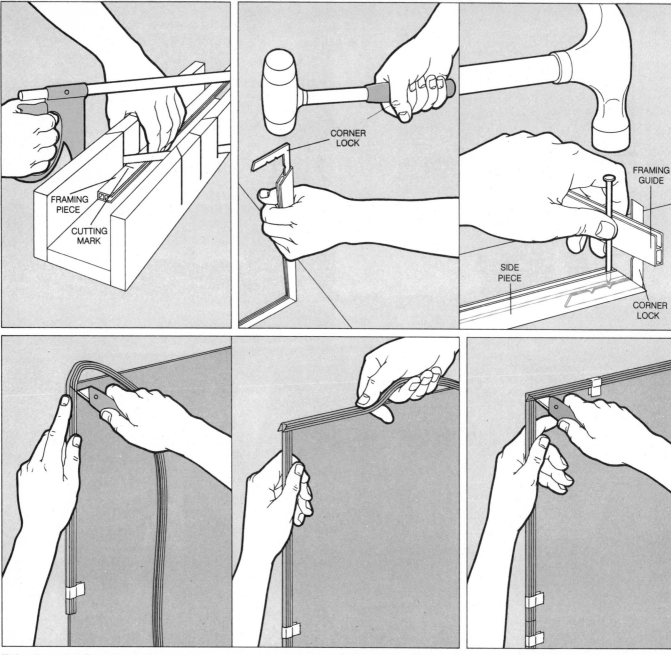

3 **Fitting the gasket.** Panes for aluminum storm windows should be 1¹⁄₁₆ inch shorter and narrower than the outside of the frame. After the glazing is cut, run the gasket around the pane, starting in the middle of one side. Tape the gasket in place temporarily. At each corner, cut the gasket at a 45° angle on both sides of the glass (*left*), then bend the gasket around the corner (*above*).

4 **Trimming the gasket.** When the gasket is in place all around the pane, trim all the corners at a 45° angle so the gasket does not overlap itself and lies flat on the pane.

102

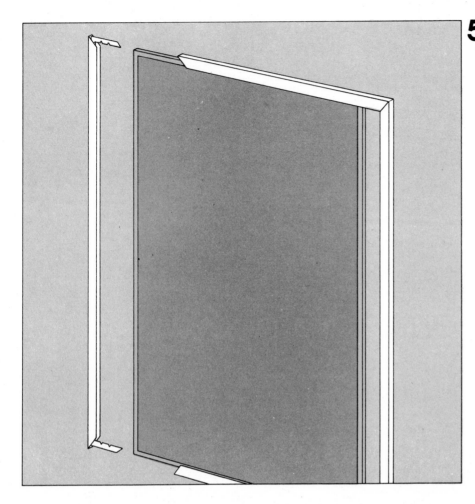

5 **Assembling pane and frame.** Slide the gasket and pane into the three-sided frame you assembled in Step 2, removing as you go the tape that is holding the gasket to the pane. Crimp corner locks into the fourth piece of the frame and slide it into position over the exposed edge of the pane. The fourth frame piece cannot be fastened to the rest of the frame because of the pane; it is the side to remove when replacing a broken pane.

Hanging Storm Windows

BRACKET
TOP

BRACKET
BOTTOM

EYE   HOOK

Mounting the brackets and hook. A pair of two-piece brackets are used to hang both wood and aluminum storm windows. Screw the bottom half of each bracket to the top of the storm window frame, 1 inch from each corner. Use wood screws for wood frames and sheet-metal screws for aluminum frames. Hold the storm window in place against the house and mark the locations for the top half of each bracket at the top of the window casing, then mount the other section of each bracket (inset). Both halves of the brackets have elongated screw slots to adjust the position of the storm window. After hanging the window, add a hook and eye to latch the bottom of the storm window closed, being careful when drilling through the frame not to hit the glass.

Storm Windows That Fit Inside

Standard storm windows that mount on the outside of a window are not practical in all situations. Bay windows, for example, may be so constructed that fitting exterior storm windows is impossible, and even if standard storm windows can be fitted to such off-sized windows, they will inevitably detract from the windows' appearance.

In such a situation, the best solution may be interior storm windows. Made of rigid clear plastic, they are available in kits that include a plastic frame *(right)*, or they can be made at home from scratch in a version that screws directly to the window molding *(bottom)*. Either type does almost as effective a job as an exterior storm window. Because of the interior location, however, condensation can form on the inside of the pane facing the existing window. Since the water can damage both paint and wood, the plastic pane may have to be taken out periodically to remove the condensation.

Assembling and Installing a Ready-made Window

1 Cutting the pane. For a tight, draft-free seal, the framed storm window should be wide enough so that its edges overlap flat areas on the existing window molding. Measure the width between flat areas. Measure the height the same way unless there is a sill. In that case measure to the top of the sill. From these measurements subtract twice the width of the mounting frame, and use the results as dimensions for the pane.

Use a grease pencil to mark these dimensions on the plastic sheet for cutting. Place the sheet on a nonabrasive surface and, with a straight length of board as a guide, use a sharp knife to score each cutting line several times from edge to edge. Snap the sheet along the scored lines.

2 Making the frame. Cut four pieces of frame material to fit around the panes, making side pieces longer than top and bottom pieces. If the window has a sill, cut the bottom piece from the sill framing *(inset)* supplied in the kit. Snap the pieces of frame material to the edges of the glazing.

Strip the protective tape from the frame's adhesive backing. Center the bottom of the new window on the sill or bottom molding of the existing window and press firmly. Working upward, position the frame so that it sticks to the window trim. Once the frame is attached, the pane can be removed by snapping open the frame.

WINDOW

SIDE FRAMING

SILL FRAMING

Custom-building a Window

Cutting the pane. Cut ¼-inch-thick rigid clear plastic to the dimensions of the window trim as measured in Step 1 at top; do not allow for a frame. If the existing window has no sill, drill pilot holes for 1-inch wood screws around the entire perimeter of the pane, ½ inch from the edge and 8 inches apart. If the window has a sill, drill holes only along the top and sides of the pane.

If there is no window sill, stick adhesive-backed weather stripping around the entire back of the pane, alongside the edges. If the window has a sill, attach weather stripping along the top and sides; for the base, stick it to the bottom edge so the cushion fits between pane and sill *(inset)*. Hold the pane against the window molding and screw it to the molding with 1-inch wood screws. When the window is removed for the summer, fill the screw holes with wood furniture plugs, available in most hardware stores. The plugs can be painted the color of the window trim.

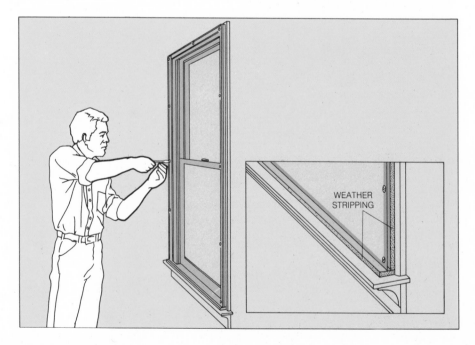

WEATHER STRIPPING

Installing a Storm Door

Even a complete system of storm windows cannot totally seal a house from wind and cold unless outer doorways are similarly protected by storm doors. Fitting a storm door is easy because most come hinged in an aluminum frame. To install the assembly you need only caulk and screw the frame to the existing doorframe; you do not have to put in hinges and hang the door. If the doorframe is not a standard size, buy a storm door slightly smaller than the frame and build out the jamb with a strip of wood.

Determine the size door assembly you need (*right*) and whether it should be hinged on the left or right—both types are available. It is best to hinge a storm door on the same side as the existing door hinges, so both need be opened as little as possible when passing through. Most storm doors have panes of safety glass or plastic; check local building codes to see which is acceptable.

1 **Measuring the doorframe.** To find the size door you need, measure the width of the doorway from jamb to jamb. Then measure the height from the threshold to the head jamb. Storm doors are available in sizes to fit standard doorways, generally 2½ to 3 feet wide and 6 feet, 8 inches high. After buying the door assembly, check its fit before going further: the shape of the threshold may interfere with the fit of the frame base. If necessary, cut the rear corners of the frame base with a hacksaw so that it fits flush with the threshold (*inset*).

2 **Caulking the doorframe.** Once the storm door and frame assembly correctly fit the existing frame, remove it and set it aside. Where the door-jamb and doorstop of the existing frame meet, apply a line of butyl rubber caulking around the entire frame. Apply a line of caulking around the extreme outer edge of the doorjamb (*inset*).

3 **Installing the storm door.** Set the door and frame assembly into the existing frame so the back fits into the frame where the jamb and stop meet. Press it firmly into place to spread the caulking, then screw the side of the frame to the doorjamb through the holes provided.

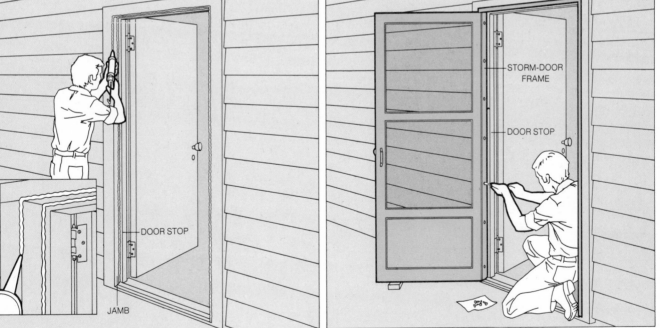

Thwarting the Sun with Awnings and Shields

Few settings are as inviting as a room dappled with sunshine. Yet too much sun can quickly turn a house into a hot-box, causing rugs and furniture to fade and creating unpleasant glare.

How can you block unwanted sunshine? Brightly colored canvas awnings, once a symbol of gracious summer living, were long the favored way. Then air conditioners permitted less cumbersome interior solutions—window hangings like curtains, blinds and shades. With the rising cost of electricity, however, awnings have made a comeback. Awnings reflect heat before it has a chance to enter, and cool more effectively than shades or curtains, which may actually absorb heat and trap it indoors. Used alone, awnings lower interior temperatures by 8° to 15°; used with air conditioning, they markedly reduce power consumption.

When you are choosing awnings, carefully consider the material they are made of. Canvas is least expensive, but it fades, tends to shrink and does not resist fire. More practical—though more costly—are awnings made of coated cottons or synthetics. Vinyl-coated, 100 per cent spun polyester lasts longer than plain canvas and has greater resistance to both fire and mildew. More durable still are awnings made of fiberglass or aluminum, which, with proper care, should serve for about 20 years.

The color of an awning is important to its efficiency. White fabric awnings, tested on the south side of a house over plate-glass windows, have proved nearly 10 per cent more effective than dark-green ones. Style, too, has practical as well as esthetic value. Awnings with sides—called wings—guard windows from peripheral sun, but they also trap heat and slow the release of warm air from inside the house. Roll-up awnings, which can be raised or lowered according to the sun's position, offer advantages over the fixed variety, which permanently block both light and view.

On the following pages are installation procedures for typical, ready-made fabric or aluminum awnings. They come in standard sizes—the measurements below indicate the minimum size you should buy—and are purchased in kits including all the hardware necessary for installa-tion on wooden window casings. When mounting on mortar or brick, be sure to use lead anchors into which wood screws can be threaded. Since details vary considerably depending on the size, style and brand of awning, read the manufacturer's instructions carefully.

If the cost or appearance of awnings makes them undesirable, an alternative is a tinted plastic film applied with water to the inner side of window glass. Depending on the brand, this shield may be held in place either by self-adhesion or by electrostatic pressure (the same force that causes a briskly rubbed balloon to adhere to a wall). These shields deflect heat so well that, in some cases, air-conditioning needs are cut by half. The film reduces visibility only slightly, and virtually eliminates glare and the ultra-violet rays that cause furnishings to fade. This method has only two major disadvantages: it lowers the daytime light level in a room, and when windows are opened to admit breezes, sunlight pours in unchecked. But the ease of installation and low price make tinted film a practical solution for many homeowners.

Measuring for Awnings

Double-hung windows. To determine the length of the awning drop, measure from the top of the window casing to a point halfway down the window. For awnings with wings, also measure the width of the window from midpoint to midpoint of the side casings. Wingless awnings should be wider; for these, measure the width of the window sash, then add 8 inches.

Casement windows. For casement windows, measure the projection—the distance from the wall to the outermost point on the window when it is fully opened—then measure the drop and width as you would for double-hung windows. Casement awnings usually are mounted higher than double-hung types. Retailers have charts to help you make the appropriate adjustment.

Installing Canvas Awnings

1 **Mounting the hardware.** Over the window, center the rod that will stiffen the awning top. Hold it level and mark its position with a drawn line. Measure in 5 inches from each end of the line to mark the positions for the head-rod holders. Next, mark the positions for the arm hinges by measuring down from the ends of the line a distance equal to the awning drop length. Install the head-rod holders, and, an inch beneath each, mount an eye screw. Install the hinges, and place the cord cleat beneath one hinge.

Turn the thumbscrew on each head-rod holder so that the metal projection points up. Hang two pulleys from the eye screw that is nearest the cleat and one pulley from the other eye screw. Close the eye screws with pliers.

2 **Hanging the awning.** Insert the front and arm bars into the appropriate pockets of the awning and connect them. Insert the head rod into the hem at the top of the awning, then lift the awning onto the hooks of the head-rod holders. Turn the thumbscrew on each holder so that the metal projection turns downward, clamping the awning *(inset)*. Tighten the thumbscrews. Remove the pin from each hinge, and place the end of the arm into the hinge. Reinsert the pin.

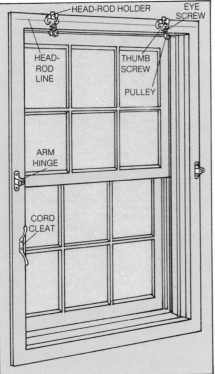

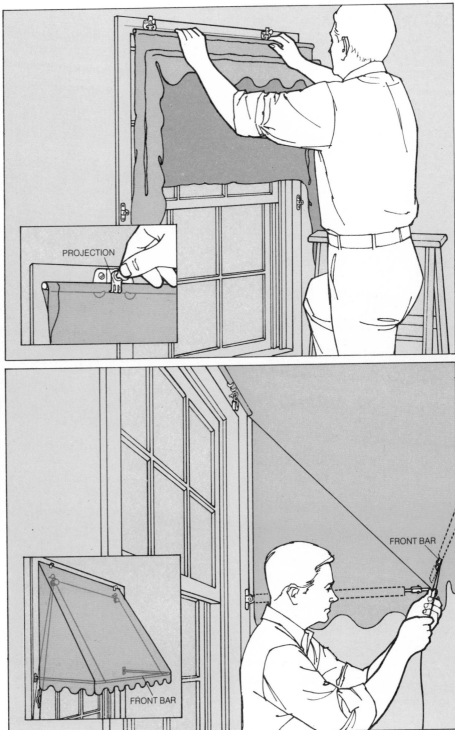

3 **Roping the awning.** Tie one end of the cord to the front bar at the pocket opening farthest from the cleat. Thread the other end first through the pulley hanging directly above, then through either of the two pulleys on the opposite side. Loop the cord around the cleat, then lead the cord through the remaining pulley and down to the front bar. Tie the end of the cord to the front bar at the pocket opening nearest the cleat *(inset)*.

Installing Aluminum Awnings

1 **Positioning the hanger strip.** To protect an aluminum awning's finish and to make mounting easier, the awning should be left rolled until it has been fastened in place. This will require removal of a metal hanger strip usually supplied in position on a track at the awning top. Start by tearing just enough of the wrapping to expose the hanger strip. Slip off the rubber bands that keep the curtain rolled and slide the strip off its track. Center the strip, with the curled edge facing down, over the window 4 inches above the sash. Holding the strip level, mark on the window casing or wall the location of the strip's ends and each of its fastener holes, as shown below. Slide the strip back onto its track, locking it in place with screws inserted into each end of the strip's curl, or follow the manufacturer's instructions. Slip the rubber bands over the roll again.

2 **Installing the hardware.** Halfway down the window, install the arm hinges so they are aligned 1 inch outside the marks designating the ends of the hanger strip. Under the window, 5 inches inside the hinges and a minimum of 30 inches below them, mark positions for two eye screws. Install the screws so their openings are vertical. Install the cleat next to either eye screw. Hang a plastic ring from each eye screw, and close the screws with pliers. At the top of the window, drill pilot holes at each of the fastener marks. If the surface is masonry or brick, use lead anchors.

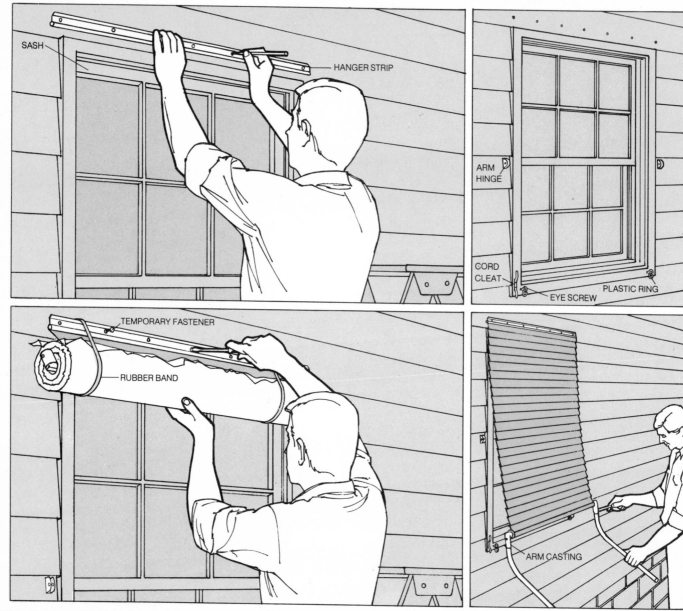

SASH

HANGER STRIP

ARM HINGE

CORD CLEAT

EYE SCREW

PLASTIC RING

TEMPORARY FASTENER

RUBBER BAND

ARM CASTING

3 **Hanging the curtain.** Align the rolled awning with the screw holes at the top of the window. Insert two temporary screws through the fastener holes in the hanger strip to the right and left of center. Turn these temporary screws so that they are secure enough to support the awning but are not fully tightened. Insert permanent screws in the remaining holes, placing a washer between the hanger strip and the screwhead. When these screws are nearly tight, remove the two temporary ones, then reinsert them with washers. Snip the restraining rubber bands and carefully unroll the awning. Tighten all the screws in the hanger strip. Remove the wrapping from the curtain.

4 **Inserting the arm.** At one end of the front tube, insert the short end of one curved arm into the arm casting. Adjust the arm so that the peak of its curve points toward the wall, and screw the arm to the casting. Install the other arm, then place the free end of each arm into its hinge and insert the hinge pins.

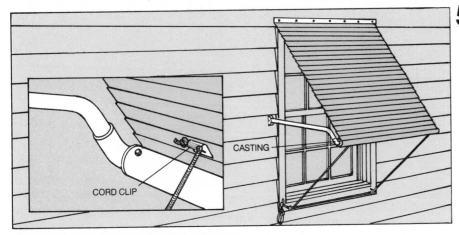

5 Installing the rope. Slide the cord clips, found near the bottom edge of the curtain, so that they are vertically aligned with the eye screws beneath the window. Tie a knot in each end of the cord, then slip one knotted end into the clip farthest from the cleat (*inset*). Pass the free end of the cord through the plastic ring on the eye screw below, then into the other clip. Loop the rope and push the loop through the remaining plastic ring. Wrap the loop securely around the cleat. Remove the locking nails from the castings at each end of the front tube to release the awning's roller springs. Unwrap the cord; let the awning roll slowly against the window frame. Equalize the tension so the awning unrolls evenly; knot the loop to maintain that balance.

Plastic Sunglasses for Windows

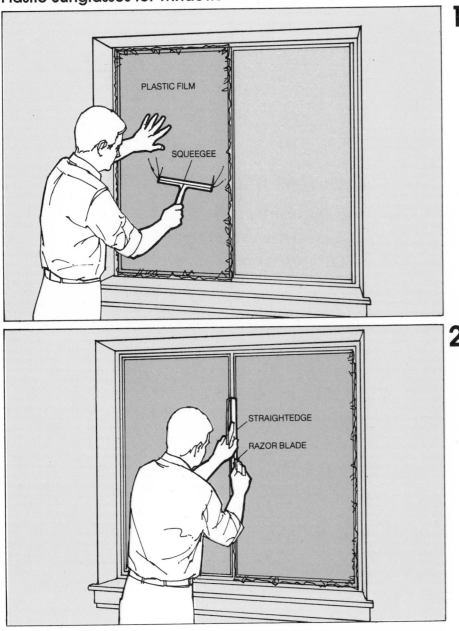

1 Preparing the window. Wash the inside of the window thoroughly. Scrape off adhering grit with a razor blade and wash the glass again. Cut the plastic film slightly larger than the glass. Mist the glass with water, peel the protective liner from the film, and mist the side of the film that will rest against the window. Apply the film to the glass, mist and lightly squeegee the surface.

2 Trimming the film. Butt a straightedge against the window sash, with the edge on the glass. Using a razor blade, trim the film along the straightedge, thus creating a narrow border of glass around the film. Mist the film again, and squeegee from the top down to remove as much water as possible from beneath the film. Finish by drying the edges of the glass with a lint-free cloth. The window will be hazy until all moisture trapped behind the film evaporates by way of the narrow border around the film's perimeter—a process that may take more than a week.

4

Defending a House from Disaster

Threatening thunderbolts. Lightning strikes some part of the earth's surface 100 times each second with a stroke that may carry over 200,000 amperes of electricity—enough current to light a quarter million 100-watt bulbs. Against such odds, a homeowner's best bet is to get an expertly installed protection system—the modern version of yesterday's lightning rods.

Besides preparing for weather's usual vagaries, homeowners everywhere must be ready for natural disasters of one sort or another: blizzards and ice storms in the North, red winds or Santa Anas in the Southwest, hurricanes along the Gulf and Atlantic coasts, earthquakes along the Pacific Coast. Tornadoes cut destructive swaths at least once a year through every state except Alaska and Rhode Island; the annual average for Texas is 108, for Oklahoma 53, for Kansas 46. And no part of the United States or Canada is completely free from the threat of seasonal or flash floods, or of thunderstorms and the lightning that accompanies them. Floods drive about 75,000 Americans from their homes each year, killing 90 persons and destroying or damaging over $250 million worth of property. Lightning kills about 150 Americans each year and injures 250; annual property loss is estimated at more than $100 million.

To protect life and property from such climatic calamities, both the United States and Canada have established storm forecasting services. Under these systems a storm or flood "watch" ("advisory" in Canada) cautions the public about the possibility of trouble, and a "warning" alerts them when the storm or flood is imminent and shelter must be sought at once. Unfortunately, not very many flash floods can be predicted in advance and earthquakes are difficult to forecast—although warnings are broadcast for the tidal waves that frequently follow their tremors.

Aside from updating your homeowner's insurance and adding policies for contingencies it may not cover, you can use your carpentry skills to safeguard the house against the most likely disasters. A simple wooden cover, made like a shadow box out of 2-by-4s and plywood *(pages 112-113),* will protect a picture window from the grab bag of trash a hurricane or tornado might fling against the glass. You can get the cover ready months before storm season and put it over the window in a matter of minutes any time a hurricane or tornado watch is announced.

With more effort you can permanently brace the inside of your roof *(page 50)* to keep it from being blown off in a high wind or crushed under heavy snow or ice. Or you can strap your chimney with metal bands *(pages 115-117)* to prevent it from pounding against the house or collapsing in an earthquake. Providing real protection from thunderstorms, however, is not a do-it-yourself project; you need a lightning protection system contractor as explained on page 118. And when nearby rivers or streams go on a rampage all you can do is to try to minimize the damage by turning off utilities and moving possessions upstairs beforehand and then cleaning and drying the house as quickly as possible afterward *(page 120).*

Windproofing a Picture Window

Pushing with 55 pounds of pressure on every square foot of a surface it strikes, a 100-mile-an-hour wind drives debris before it like missiles. Window glass is no match for that kind of force. If you live in a place where powerful winds are a threat, you must be ready to cover all windows quickly at the first warning.

Shutters serve to protect small windows, but picture windows usually are too large to shutter—and simply nailing boards across them may damage the frame or siding. For first-floor picture windows, which are the most common sort, the type of plywood cover illustrated on these pages offers complete protection. The cover fits between the sill and the drip cap outside the casing so that it cannot scratch the glass. Angled 2-by-4s, anchored to the ground by stakes, hold the cover firmly.

Because the cover is designed as a knockdown, you can build it at any time and store it, ready for quick assembly, until you need to use it.

Building a Window Cover

1 **Measuring the window.** Measure the exterior height of the window from the bottom of the drip cap to the top of the sill. Measure the width from the outer edge of one side casing to the outer edge of the other. For the length of the supports, measure from the bottom of the drip cap to the ground and multiply this figure by 1½.

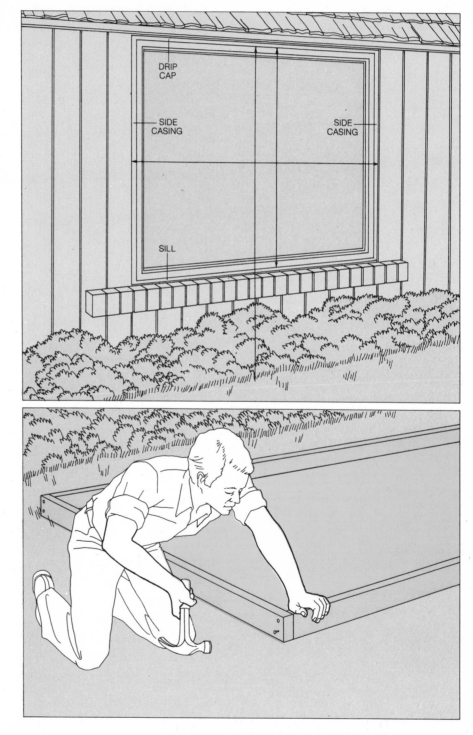

2 **Assembling the cover.** To make the cover, cut ½-inch plywood to the dimensions determined in Step 1, if necessary piecing two panels together with wood battens. To frame it, make a rectangle of 2-by-4s the size of the plywood and butt-nail it with 3½-inch nails. Secure the plywood to the frame with 1¼-inch nails at 6- to 8-inch intervals.

3 Attaching supports. Cut two 2-by-4s to the length determined in Step 1. Then stand the cover on its side and place one support in the upper corner of the frame at a 45° angle. Hold the support level with a scrap of 2-by-4. Bore a ⅜-inch hole through both support and frame. Label the holes with a letter or number so you can identify and match them later. Turn the cover onto the opposite side and repeat the process.

4 Fitting the cover. Stand the cover, frame side out, in front of the window, using sawhorses or trash cans to help hold it. Set the supports in place and, using the holes bored in Step 3, secure them with nuts and ¼-inch bolts, 4 inches long. Position the cover against the window. Set the cover on the sill and measure from the bottom corner of the frame to the far edge of one support to find the length for bottom braces. Take the cover down, unbolt the supports and cut two 1-by-3-inch bottom braces.

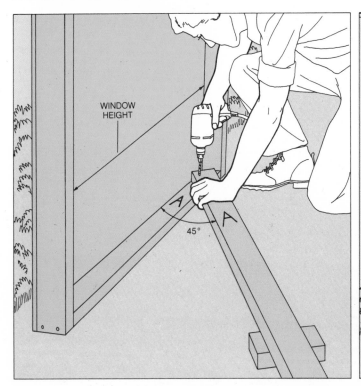

Final Steps before the Storm

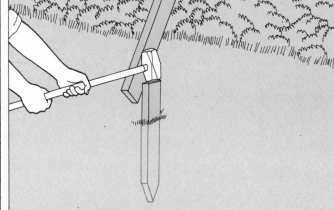

1 Bracing the cover. Follow the procedure in Step 4 (*top right*) to bolt the supports to the frame and fit the cover over the window. Using double-headed nails 2 inches long (they are easy to remove later), fasten a brace between each lower corner of the frame and the adjacent support.

2 Anchoring the supports. Drive a pointed stake 18 inches long deeply into the ground beside the base of each support. Use double-headed nails 3½ inches long to nail the stake to the support.

Tying Down a Mobile Home

Perched on its I-beam undercarriage, a mobile home is imperiled by all kinds of windstorms. A hurricane or tornado can lift the home right off its footings unless it is secured with metal cables or straps that tie the undercarriage to the ground. And because such a home is generally off-balance—with all the heavy appliances strung along one wall—even a 50-mile-an-hour gale can roll it over unless there are additional ties across the roof.

Mobile homes are now manufactured with invisible roof ties built in under the top surface and with frame-tie cables attached to the I beams, all ready to be fastened to turnbuckles and anchored. For older homes, the roof ties must be hung over the outside of the structure and rings must be welded to the beams—or holes for eyebolts drilled into the beams *(bottom, right)*—to provide a place to fasten the frame ties. The cables are held by concrete posts or by auger anchors—large metal rods with screw ends that are turned into the ground, gripping it firmly. Most homes must have at least two roof ties, located no more than 5 feet from each end, plus a pair of frame ties for every 10 feet or so of overall length. In areas where high winds are frequent, roof ties should be matched to frame ties at 10-foot intervals.

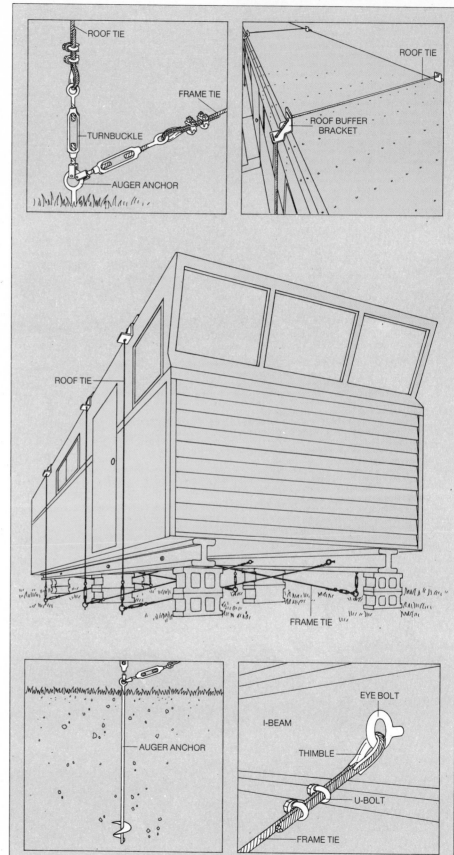

A windproofed home. A properly protected mobile home is held by turnbuckle-adjusted ¼-inch cables that run over buffer brackets on the roof or through eye bolts in the undercarriage before being secured to auger anchors.

Chimney Ties for Earth Tremors

While a solidly built wood frame house stands an excellent chance of surviving an earthquake, one with an exterior masonry chimney does not. When the ground starts shaking, the house and chimney tend to behave as separate structures, pounding against each other or pulling apart.

To prevent chimneys from collapsing and destroying houses, most new homes in areas subject to quakes have steel reinforced masonry attached to the frame with built-in steel ties. On older homes, chimneys can be safeguarded with exterior metal bands secured to the joists between the floors as shown below. The bands, which are made of 3/16-by-1¼-inch strap iron or steel strapping, can be cut and shaped with hand tools and a vise—or fabricated to fit by a metal supply or welding house. Drilling holes in the straps and installing them calls for a ½-inch electric drill with ¼- and ½-inch bits—and 3/8-by-3-inch lag bolts.

1 Planning the first-floor strap. To position the strap horizontally on the first-floor header joist, measure inside the house from the top casing of a window near the chimney to the ceiling; add 2½ inches. Outside the house, mark this distance above the window. Using a carpenter's level, draw a line around the chimney, extending about 3 feet on either side. To determine the length for the strap, measure the perimeter of the chimney at the line and add 6 feet. If there is no window nearby, drive a nail 6 inches long through the wall at the top corner of the ceiling beside the chimney. Mark the exterior or 2½ inches above the tip of the nail. Remove the nail and patch the hole. Draw a horizontal line at the mark as described above.

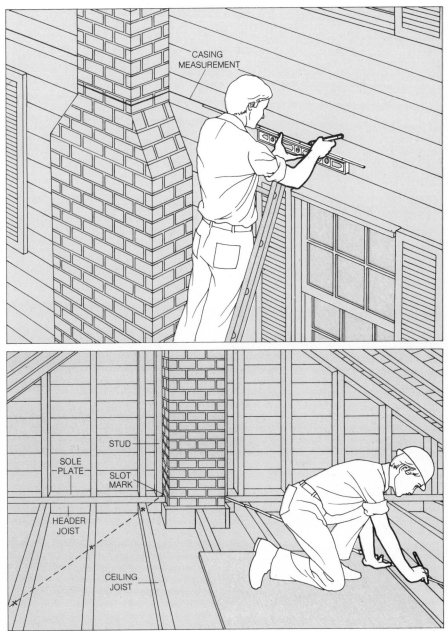

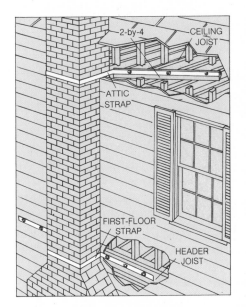

Tying a chimney to a house. Metal straps wrapped around the chimney are secured to the header joist between the first and second floors, and to the ceiling joists in the attic. Because trouble starts at the top, the attic strap is inserted through the exterior wall and attached to 2-by-4s laid diagonally across three joists. In a finished attic, this will require rebuilding the floor at a higher level to cover the strap.

2 Planning the attic strap. If the chimney is exposed in the attic, mark the locations for the wall slots by drawing a 1¾-inch vertical line above the sole plate at each side of the chimney—between the nearest stud and the exposed masonry. To determine the strap length, lay the ruler at a 45° angle away from the stud toward the outside wall at one slot mark. Extend the ruler across three ceiling joists.

Double this length and add the outside perimeter of the chimney plus 1 foot to figure total length of the strap.

If the chimney is not exposed in the attic, you can determine the locations for the slots by driving a nail through the wall beside the chimney from the exterior. The top of the header will be about level with the bottom of the eaves.

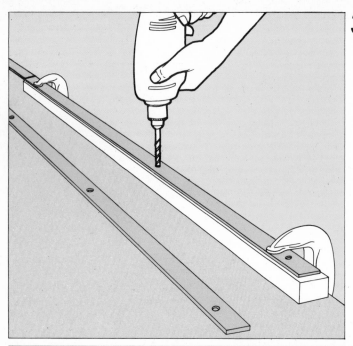

3 **Making the straps.** Wearing goggles, cut both straps to length with a hacksaw. For the first-floor strap, use a nail to scribe a pair of lines across the width 3 feet inside each end and another pair of lines inside the first set at a distance equal to ¼ inch less than the side measurement of the chimney. With a ½-inch high-speed bit in a ½-inch drill, bore three holes at each end of the strap—one 2 inches from the end, another 2 inches outside the first line, the third midway between.

For the attic strap, scribe a pair of lines at a distance from each end equal to the diagonal measurement made in Step 2, page 115, and a second pair inside the first set at a distance equal to the exterior side measurement of the chimney plus 6 inches. Drill three holes at each end—one 2 inches from the end, the second 2 inches inside the first line and the third midway between.

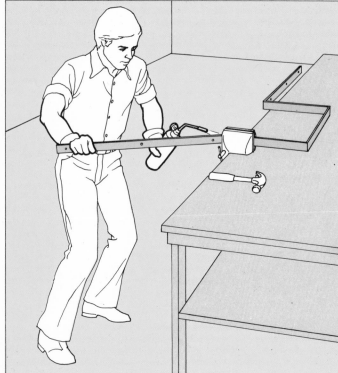

4 **Shaping the straps.** For the first-floor strap, clamp the metal band into a vise with the first scribe line set at the edge of the jaws. Holding a propane torch at the scribe line, bend the end back along the line with your hands to form a sharp 90° angle. Turning the strap over each time to reverse the direction of the bend, make 90° angles at the three remaining scribe lines. For the attic strap, make 90° angles at the inner pair of scribe lines, turning the strap so the angles create a U-shape.

5 **Installing the first-floor strap.** Hold the strap against the walls on both sides of the chimney, aligning the bottom to the line drawn in Step 1, page 115. Make a mark at each hole in the strap before taking it down. Then, with the ½-inch electric drill and a ¼-inch bit, drill holes through the wall into the header joist at each mark. Using a socket or crescent wrench, secure the strap with ⅜-by-3-inch lag bolts with washers.

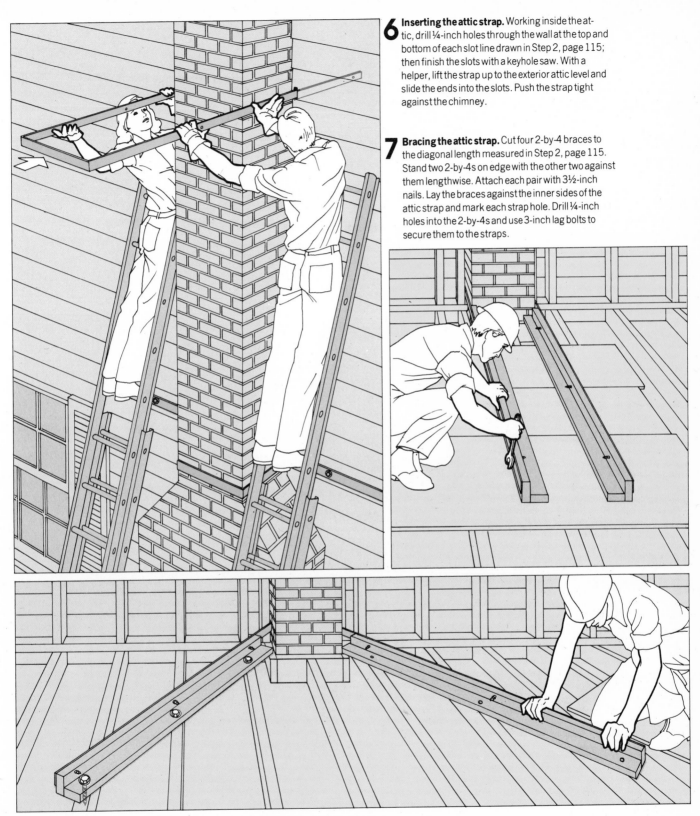

6 **Inserting the attic strap.** Working inside the attic, drill ¼-inch holes through the wall at the top and bottom of each slot line drawn in Step 2, page 115; then finish the slots with a keyhole saw. With a helper, lift the strap up to the exterior attic level and slide the ends into the slots. Push the strap tight against the chimney.

7 **Bracing the attic strap.** Cut four 2-by-4 braces to the diagonal length measured in Step 2, page 115. Stand two 2-by-4s on edge with the other two against them lengthwise. Attach each pair with 3½-inch nails. Lay the braces against the inner sides of the attic strap and mark each strap hole. Drill ¼-inch holes into the 2-by-4s and use 3-inch lag bolts to secure them to the straps.

8 **Anchoring the attic strap.** To bend each end of the strap at a 45° angle, press the brace away from the chimney, using the stud next to the chimney as a leverage point. Nail the braces temporarily to the ceiling joists. Then drill ½-inch holes through the braces where they cross each joist but do not drill into the joists. With the ¼-inch bit, drill the holes another 1½ inches deep. Insert 3-inch lag bolts with washers; remove the nails. Fill the gap at the wall slots with caulking.

Warding Off Lightning Damage

Safeguarding a home from the million or more volts of a lightning flash calls for a professional contractor, not just because only he has the expertise and special equipment necessary to install and test the system, but, more important, because an improperly installed system is likely to pose a greater hazard to your home than no protection at all. But there are some things you can do yourself.

Make sure that wiring and appliances are protected from lightning-surge damage—the powerful currents that can run into the house through overhead power lines or antenna cables when lightning strikes in the area. Such currents are diverted to the ground by lightning arresters or surge protectors, installed at the main fuse or circuit-breaker panel and on the television antenna lead-in. Installing an arrester on the power lines is a job for an expert—it requires working on hot wires from the utility lines in the street —but attaching an arrester to the antenna lead-in wire is a simple screwdriver job *(opposite bottom)*. The arrester shown is designed for use with a 300-ohm flat lead-in; arresters for 75-ohm coaxial cable are also available. In either case, the arrester should carry the Underwriters' Laboratories (UL) seal.

The antenna mast itself should also be grounded; if it is not, connect it to a grounded water pipe *(opposite top)*. Clamps and wire for mast grounding, as well as lead-in arresters, are available at electrical and electronic-supply stores.

Remember that these measures do not provide adequate lightning protection in the event of a direct strike to your home or antenna; only a professionally designed system with heavy-gauge conductors and alternate paths to ground *(below)* can afford that safety. But these measures may prevent a burn-out of expensive electrical equipment.

Although surge arresters and antenna grounds are advisable everywhere, not every home needs a full-scale lightning protection system. One should be considered, however, if you live in an area of frequent thunderstorms such as central Florida or the thunderstorm belts of the Southeast or Midwest; in New England, thunderstorms occur less frequently but are often very severe. If your home is the tallest and largest in the neighborhood (a tall metal antenna effectively raises the roof height) or if it is isolated, it is more likely to be hit since it will be the dominant structure in the area.

If you do decide to have a complete protection system, insist that the installation conform to the standards of the National Fire Protection Association and the Underwriters' Laboratories. When the job is completed, UL-certified installers will submit an application, witnessed by the homeowner, for a UL Master Label. This label, actually a brass plate affixed to the equipment, certifies that the system has been professionally installed and subjects it to spot-checking by UL field inspectors. The Master Label may entitle you to a rate reduction on your homeowner's insurance policy.

After the system is installed, inspect it annually. Check for bent, loose or missing air terminals, as well as breaks or fraying in the conductors; make certain clamps and splices are tight, and that no new construction near the house has damaged the buried rods and cable.

A lightning protection system. In a professional installation, thin, pointed rods called air terminals are placed along the high points of the roof —ridge, dormers and chimney—where they will intercept a direct lightning strike. A main conductor of heavy-gauge copper or aluminum cable joins the terminals to one another and to at least two copper ground rods driven into the earth at diagonally opposite corners of the house.

Prominent metal objects on the roof, such as the television antenna, are connected to the main conductor; other large metal objects within 6 feet of the main cable, such as the plumbing system's vent pipe, gutters and downspouts, and metal flashings, are connected with smaller-gauge branch conductors. Another branch conductor enters the basement to tie in the plumbing, electrical and telephone systems.

Any tree taller than the house and located within 10 feet of the foundation should be protected with special tree terminals—not only to protect the tree, but to guard the house against side-flashes that might leap from the tree if it is struck.

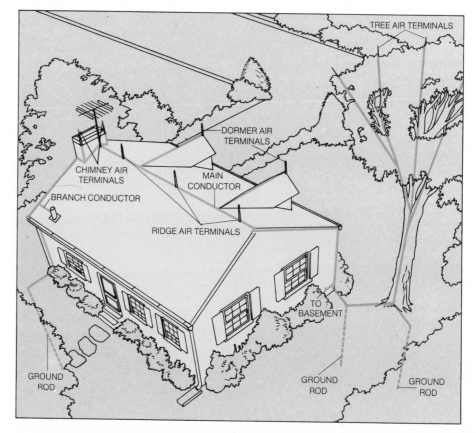

Protection for Television Sets

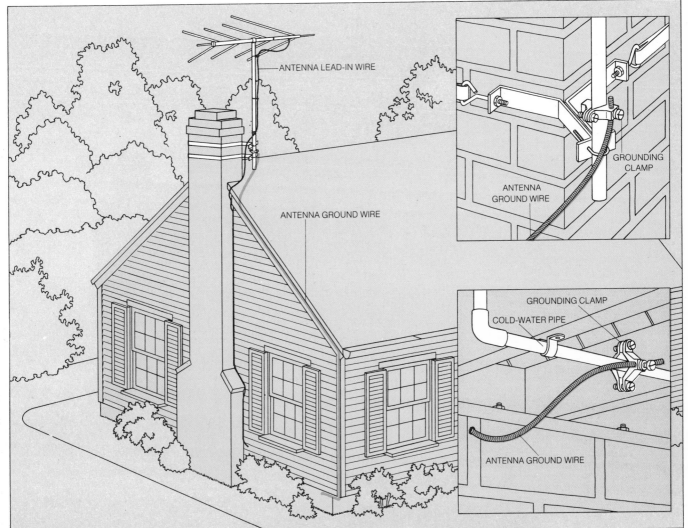

ANTENNA LEAD-IN WIRE

ANTENNA GROUND WIRE

GROUNDING CLAMP

ANTENNA GROUND WIRE

GROUNDING CLAMP

COLD-WATER PIPE

ANTENNA GROUND WIRE

Grounding the antenna. Attach a length of No. 8 aluminum or No. 10 copper wire to the mast with a grounding clamp (*inset, top*), checking to make certain that the ground wire is securely held in the clamp. Run the wire along the eave and down the siding, securing it every 3 to 4 feet with staples. Use another grounding clamp to attach the other end of the cable to a metal cold-water pipe in the basement (*inset, bottom*).

Installing the lightning arrester. Attach the arrester to the antenna lead-in wire at the lowest possible point—where it will be close to a good ground connection—generally near the point where the lead-in enters the house. Lay the lead-in into the groove on the face of the arrester and tighten the wing nuts on each terminal so that the serrated washers penetrate the insulation and make contact with the wires (*right*). Mount the arrester, using the mounting strap and wood screws provided. Attach a wire to the ground terminal and clamp it to a grounded water pipe.

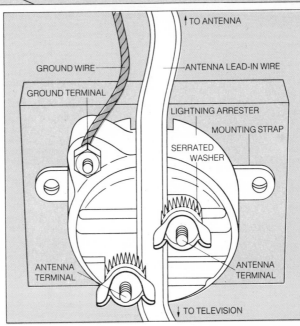

TO ANTENNA

GROUND WIRE

ANTENNA LEAD-IN WIRE

GROUND TERMINAL

LIGHTNING ARRESTER

MOUNTING STRAP

SERRATED WASHER

ANTENNA TERMINAL

ANTENNA TERMINAL

TO TELEVISION

Coping with the Chaos of a Flood

There is not much you can do to keep a flood out of your house when a river engulfs it. If you live in a place where such an occurrence is a possibility by all means avail yourself of the federally subsidized flood insurance that can now be purchased. If you have some advance warning—as you probably will—you can limit damage to some extent. And after the flood there are a number of things you can do to speed the cleanup job.

When the radio alert becomes a clear warning of impending disaster, move upstairs as much furniture, bedding, clothing, kitchenware and food as you can. Stow away plastic jugs and pots of water.

Then throw the main cutoff switch for the electricity and close the main valve to protect the water already in your system. Switch off the furnace and hot-water heater, the valve to the oil tank, and all appliances through the house. Just before you lock the doors and leave, open the basement windows so water can enter there to equalize the outside pressure and prevent cave-ins.

After the flood, when local authorities advise that it is safe to return, go back by daylight. Watch out for fallen electric lines, leaking gas or oil, and inflammable or explosive materials from upstream.

Reenter only after you ascertain that the foundation and walls are sound. Inside, watch for buckling, nails or holes underfoot and for loose plaster overhead. Break down sagging ceilings with a stick. If the house passes your safety inspection, start the drying and cleaning process by opening all doors, windows and vents, and bailing out water from the upper floors. Leave the basement alone until all the water standing outside it recedes. Then rent or borrow a gasoline-powered pump to empty the water from the basement into the street. Reduce the level gradually—2 or 3 feet a day. Pumping too soon, or too fast, may make the walls collapse or the floor heave. When pumping is complete, call on professionals to restore utilities and restart the furnace and appliances.

Cleaning the house, however, is a job you can do for yourself—and the sooner you start the better. Moving furniture from room to room or outdoors as you go, remove the silt deposit and debris from floors and walls as shown here. As soon as water is available, flush out the silt residue with a hose, then wash and disinfect the house and its contents. After that you probably can move back in, but you must delay repainting and refinishing until everything is dry—a process that may take weeks or months.

1 **Scraping up mud.** Clear out the furnishings and large pieces of debris. Then push the accumulated mud and small debris away from the walls toward a window or exterior door with a shovel or a squeegee made by fitting a length of garden hose over the teeth of a rake.

2 **Disposing of mud.** Nail together two 1-by-12s 6 or 7 feet long to form a V-shaped trough. Prop up one end on a window sill, extending the trough outdoors. Then nail a 2-by-4 under the outside end to hold the trough at an incline so you can slide the mud and debris down it.

Remove the carpeting and tackless strips under it, and the rugs or any loose tiles from the floor. After water service is restored, hose the silt residue from the floors and scrub them with household detergent and disinfectant.

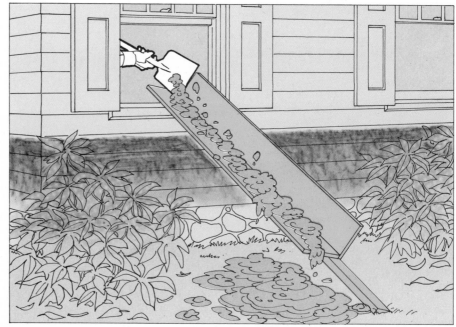

Cleaning and Drying Walls

1 **Breaking wet walls.** Break away water-soaked wallboard or plaster on the interior faces of exterior walls and along both sides of interior partitions. Break off enough so you can see the wires or pipes buried between studs. Pull out wet insulation—unless dry, it is worthless.

2 **Removing trim.** Using a utility bar, crowbar or large putty knife, pry up and remove the shoe molding nailed to the floor. Pry the baseboard partially away from the studs, then release it to expose the heads of the nails holding it in place. Pull out the nails with the bar or a hammer so you can lift the baseboard out in sections that can be replaced after washing and drying.

3 **Trimming walls.** Use a shovel to remove mud from between studs, then wash the studs and sole plate with detergent and a brush. Use a key-hole saw to cut off the bottom section of the wall about a foot above the waterline to prevent moisture from being absorbed into the top section.

After the wall is completely dry, which may take several months, replace the insulation. Cover the bottom section with new wallboard and use tape and joint compound to conceal the joints where it meets the top. If the old walls were lath and plaster, attach lath spacers to the studs to make the wallboard align with the plaster above.

A Seasonal Check List for a Snug House

Emergency repairs come at the wrong time, in the wrong weather, when tools and materials to do them properly seem to be missing. If you do not wait for the emergency but tackle each job at the appropriate time, you can make minor repairs before they become major ones. The following calendar indicates the seasons best suited for the maintenance that will keep your house weathertight.

Spring

Gutters

The weight of winter snow and ice can force gutters out of alignment or start leaks at low points. During a heavy spring rain, look for drips and points of overflow—or, in dry weather, run water through the gutters from a garden hose. Reposition nails or gutter hangers to return a gutter to the correct pitch; scrape rusted spots clean with a wire brush and coat both the rusted area and the surface immediately around it with gutter cement or asphalt-aluminum paint. A small rust hole can be stopped with an aluminum patch and a coat of gutter cement, but if a gutter is pitted with many holes or has rusted through in long seams, replace the entire run (pages 24-25).

Roofs

Repair or replace curled, split or missing shingles. Use quick-setting roofing cement, applied with a caulking gun, to reseat a curled shingle; a slightly split shingle can be reseated in the same way, then fastened down with roofing nails. If a shingle is badly damaged or rotted through, replace it completely: use a hacksaw or slate puller to remove the nails that hold it in place and substitute a new shingle or strip of shingle (pages 40-45). On a flat roof, check for blisters and make repairs before water gets through the roof sheathing. Cut each blister open, dry the underlying felt if necessary, and seal the cut with asphalt roofing cement and a felt patch (pages 46-47). Finally, remove rust spots from metal flashing with a wire brush and coat the rusted areas and the surfaces around them with primer and aluminum paint; if necessary, renew the roofing cement that seals flashing to shingles (pages 48-49).

Bird Nests

Some nests are welcome, others are dangerous. If, after migrating to your area, birds nest against an attic vent or the outer cover of a venting fan, remove the nest. Recheck the spot periodically for the remainder of the season—other birds are likely to find the same good nesting place. (A spring chore in most of the United States and Canada, it should be done in fall in the Southern states.)

Tornado Precautions

In the tornado belt—essentially, the Great Plains of the United States and Canada—take measures to protect your home and yourself before the high tornado months of May and June. Make or repair strong wooden covers for your windows (pages 112-113) and consider building a storm cellar—plans for cellars are available in free or inexpensive government publications. If you have a mobile home, anchor it to concrete posts or directly into the ground (page 114).

Lightning Protection

Before summer electrical storms begin, make your annual inspection of your lightning-protection system, but do not try to repair the system yourself—an amateur repair can be more dangerous than the defect itself. If any air terminals, ground rods, cables, conductors or clamps (pages 118-119) are loose, damaged or completely missing, have the installer repair them.

Summer

Insect Nests

By early summer, most bee and wasp nests are well established, but still small enough to be easily removed. Look for them at eaves or other under-roof areas; use binoculars on the outside of the house to check eave or soffit vents or look from inside an attic to see if insects have worked their way into the louvers of a roof or attic vent. If you find a nest, do not attempt to remove it while it is still inhabited—first kill the insects with a spray, then knock the nest down and clean the area to which it was fastened.

Vent Blockages

On a hot day you should be able to perceive rising currents of air starting at soffit vents and moving toward vents on a gable or roof, if you do not, clean the vents—they can be clogged with leaves—and make sure that the insides are not blocked by furniture stored in the attic.

Kitchen Fans

In summer grease builds up fast but is easily removed. Wash the filter, then take out the motor-and-fan assembly (in most models the assembly is secured by two or three screws and the motor can be disconnected by pulling a plug). Use a solution of household detergent to clear all surfaces of grease, but do not submerge the motor. Be very careful not to bend fan blades, which generally are thin. Before replacing the assembly, oil the motor and clean the housing.

Moisture

At points where wood meets other materials, or where a wooden structure such as a porch meets the main house, look for water damage indicated by flaking or blistered paint. (Remember that water can flow along these seams for some distance before lodging and damaging wood or paint.) Recaulk the points from which water penetrated the paint *(pages 16-19)*, but do not try to touch up the paint that still adheres directly over the moist wood. First remove the blistered or loose paint and let the wood dry thoroughly; if moisture has raised a nap on the damp wood, sand the area smooth before repainting.

Hurricane Precautions

Along the Atlantic and Gulf coasts, prepare for the high hurricane winds of early fall in much the same way that inlanders prepare for tornadoes *(see Spring: Tornado precautions)*. Both types of storm inflict the same kind of damage; hurricanes, however, give more warning of their approach, and you can usually get out of their way. If an alert does come, take a few hours to anchor outdoor objects to the ground or move them into the house. And because hurricanes may cause flooding or power failures over a large area and for a considerable length of time, store canned food and fresh water (in a bathtub, if necessary) and lay in battery-powered lights and radios—and perhaps a kerosene lantern or two.

Fall

Caulking

The freezing water of winter, which can expand inside or alongside a caulked seam, is even harder on caulks than the warm moisture of summer. Before the first frost, go over all the caulks in your house, from roof to basement *(pages 16-17)*—even a caulking material that is guaranteed for years should get this annual inspection. The spots of greatest danger, and the ones that most often need recaulking, are window wells and the frames of windows and doors.

Gutters

As the trees begin to go bare, install leaf guards on gutters and wire cages on downspouts or, if necessary, repair or replace existing guards and cages. Later in the season, clean your gutters of fallen leaves and other debris—do not count on rain to move this material, which is likely to mat up and clog your entire rain carry-off system. Use a stiff brush to get at dirt and mineral granules washed down from an asphalt-shingle roof; if necessary, dig out encrusted matter at the bottom of a gutter with a small trowel. Finally, flush the gutter out with a garden hose, and cover rust spots with a metal primer.

Weather Stripping

Like caulking, weather stripping is usually guaranteed for a period of years but should be inspected annually. The stripping itself may be perfectly sound, but settling of a house and the friction of a moving sash or door can weaken or destroy the seal. On a windy day hold a lighted match near the edges of every weather-stripped opening to see if there are leaks. Apply new stripping wherever it is needed, and adjust door saddles if necessary for a tight fit *(pages 12-15)*.

Storm Windows and Doors

Before putting up these winter necessities, wash them thoroughly—and while you are at it, wash the windows and glass inserts in the doors of the house itself to keep from sealing in films of dust and dirt during the months ahead. Storm windows and doors fitted with wooden frames may need a fresh coat of paint or a new set of metal reinforcing straps. Metal frames may need treatment for corrosion; use steel wool to clean corroded areas down to smooth bare metal, and cover these areas or the entire frame with a protective coat of paste wax. Check both wood and metal frames for warping and, if necessary, adjust the clearance and fit of doors and sill strips.

Winter

Insulation Check

Weak spots in your insulation cover are often hard to detect during the warm months of the year, but may show up clearly when snow blankets your roof. Examine the roof for bare patches or streaks—they are almost certainly places insulation has settled and matted, or where batts or blankets have been pierced or have pulled away from their fastenings. These areas of high heat loss are expensive; repair the insulation immediately. At the same time, check the attic for leaks: melting snow may have penetrated the roof, or old leaks may have soaked the insulation. Roof leaks are difficult to repair in winter, but a bad leak is so dangerous to the structure of a house that the job should be undertaken—by a professional, if necessary.

Ice Dams

Despite all precautions, snow may freeze to ice at the edge of a roof, usually starting at a clogged gutter or downspout. Snow builds up above the ice and at the first thaw—or even with the melting caused by a normal heat loss from the roof—melting snow can work its way between shingles to produce serious leaks. At least once during the winter, check the roof for ice dams; if you find any, break them up and remove them.

Termite Check

Termites in their winged stage often swarm in February; check the basement for them. Even if you do not see any, take the time for a systematic termite check. Look for small heaps of sawdust on the floor, and for the mud-walled tubes through which termites tunnel toward moisture. To check the interiors of studs and joists, drive a sharp tool—an awl or an ice pick will do—deep into the wood and work it in and out, searching for small hollows and honeycombed areas caused by termite infestation. At any sign of infestation, call in a professional exterminator immediately.

Picture Credits

The sources for the illustrations in this book are shown below. Credits for the pictures from left to right are separated by semicolons, from top to bottom by dashes.

Cover—Ken Kay. 6—Ken Kay. 8 through 11—Drawings by Whitman Studio, Inc. 12 through 15—Drawings by Nick Fasciano. 17—Drawing by Whitman Studio, Inc. 18, 19—Drawings by Peter McGinn. 20—Ken Kay. 22, 23—Drawings by Nick Fasciano. 24 through 27—Drawings by Ray Skibinski. 28, 29—Drawings by Adolph E. Brotman. 30, 31—Drawings by Nick Fasciano. 32, 33—Drawings by Adolph E. Brotman. 34 through 37—Drawings by Vantage Art, Inc. 38, 39—Drawings by Ray Skibinski. 40, 41—Drawings by Peter McGinn. 42, 43—Drawings by Nick Fasciano. 44, 45—Drawings by Whitman Studio, Inc. 46, 47—Drawings by Peter McGinn. 48, 49—Drawings by Adolph E. Brotman. 50—Drawings by Michael Flanagan. 51—Drawings by Michael Flanagan and Vantage Art, Inc. 52, 53—Drawings by Nick Fasciano. 54, 55—Drawings by Peter McGinn. 56 through 59—Drawings by Adolph E. Brotman. 60, 61—Drawings by Peter McGinn. 62, 63—Drawings by Ray Pioch. 64, 65—Drawings by Ray Skibinski. 66, 67—Drawings by Peter McGinn. 68—Ken Kay. 71, 72, 73—Drawings by Vantage Art, Inc. 74, 75—Drawings by Peter McGinn. 76, 77—Drawings by Whitman Studio, Inc. 78, 79—Drawings by Michael Flanagan. 80, 81—Drawings by Randall Lieu and Jim Silks. 82 through 85—Drawings by Vantage Art, Inc. 86, 87—Drawings by Ray Skibinski. 88, 89—Drawings by John Sagan. 90, 91—Drawings by Whitman Studio, Inc. 92, 93—Drawings by Ray Skibinski. 94, 95—Drawings by Whitman Studio, Inc. 96, 97—Drawings by Frederic F. Bigio from B-C Graphics. 98 through 103—Drawings by Peter McGinn. 104, 105—Drawings by Randall Lieu and Jim Silks. 106 through 109—Drawings by Adolph E. Brotman. 110—© John R. Clawson, National Audubon Society Collection/Photo Researchers, Inc. 112, 113—Drawings by Nick Fasciano. 114 through 117—Drawings by Ray Skibinski. 118—Drawing by Robert Ritter. 119—Drawings by Robert Ritter and Vantage Art, Inc. 120, 121—Drawings by Edward Vebell.

Acknowledgments

The index/glossary for this book was prepared by Mel Ingber. The editors also wish to thank the following: James Baker, Baker Lightning Rod Protection, Webster, New York; Ron Baumgardner, Rollin, Inc., Stroudsburg, Pennsylvania; Elizabeth and Berne S. Clarke, Wilton, Connecticut; Norman H. Davis III, Administrative Field Engineer, Underwriters Laboratories, Inc., Northbrook, Illinois; Marvin M. Frydenlund, Executive Director, Lightning Protection Institute, Harvard, Illinois; Ralph Johnson, Chicago Tent & Textile, Chicago, Illinois; Dave Lang, All-states Termite Control Company Inc., Alexandria, Virginia; John Lee, Structural Slate Company, Pen Argyl, Pennsylvania; Robert Lindquist, Thompson Lightning Protection, Inc., St. Paul, Minnesota; Kirk Loadman, Artcraft Industries, Pittsburg, Pennsylvania; Rapperswill, Inc., New York City; M. S. Rosenthal, President, St. Louis Lightning Protection Company, St. Louis, Missouri; Roy Spalthoff, 3-M Company, St. Paul, Minnesota; W. N. Sweet Jr., Woods Lightning Protection Co., Shelton, Connecticut; Karl Theiss, Associated Water Industries, Inc., Stamford, Connecticut; Edwin P. Weigel, Public Affairs Officer, National Weather Service, Silver Spring, Maryland; Ben Zale, Corporate Marketing and Services Department, GAF Corporation, New York City.

Index/Glossary

Printed in U.S.A.